Jon Whettingsteel is a partner at Dutton Gregory Solicitors. He has practiced in family law for the past 12 years and has experience in dealing with a wide variety of contentious and non-contentious matters including divorce, children and financial cases, as well as protective measures such as non-molestation and occupation order proceedings. Jon also has experience in drafting and advising on various documents, including consent orders, separation agreements and pre-nuptial agreements.

Jon has advised and represented heterosexual and same sex couples, including in applications for a Parental Order following surrogacy treatment, including in the High Court following international surrogacy.

Jon has dealt with multiple cases in the area of child relocation, including both as the applicant seeking permission to relocate and as a respondent in opposing an application.

A Practical Guide to Internal and External Child Relocation

A Practical Guide to Internal and External Child Relocation

Jonathan Whettingsteel LLB (Hons)
Partner and Family Law Solicitor
Dutton Gregory Solicitors

Law Brief Publishing

The information in this book was believed to be correct at the time of writing. All content is for information purposes only and is not intended as legal advice. No liability is accepted by either the publisher or author for any errors or omissions (whether negligent or not) that it may contain. Professional advice should always be obtained before applying any information to particular circumstances.

Published 2021 by Law Brief Publishing, an imprint of Law Brief Publishing Ltd
30 The Parks
Minehead
Somerset
TA24 8BT

www.lawbriefpublishing.com

Paperback: 978-1-914608-06-3

For Becky, I couldn't have done this without your support, and Isaac, who has given me a new purpose

PREFACE

There are some people that I'd like to thank. Firstly my Wife Rebecca. Thank you for supporting me, not just with this book but with the long hours, late nights and lost weekends working that come with doing this job. Especially thank you for being the second pair of ears to listen to my thoughts and ideas and second pair of eyes on proof reading.

Thank you to all at Dutton Gregory for the time and supporting enabling me to write this book, especially Paul Sams for suggesting I write a book in the first place, an idea that I thought was as wild and crazy as one of your shirts!

Thank you to Garry and all at Law Brief Publishing for their input, tips and time in bringing some words that I put in a computer in to a real life book.

Finally, thank you to you for taking the time to purchase and read this book. I hope that you will find this a useful guidance on the law on child relocation, both inside and outside of the UK.

The purpose of this book is to be a useful reference tool, broken down in to easily navigable sections to enable you to advise clients on the statutes, case law and procedures that apply in internal and external relocation. This should provide a complete 'go-to' guide on the law around child relocation, and should help those who have little knowledge or experience on this area of law or those who have been practicing for some time, and just want look up a particular point.

The contained information in this book was accurate as at 31 October 2021, and to the best of the writer's knowledge at that time there were no pending cases awaiting Judgement that are likely to impact upon the contents of this book and guidance contained within in.

Jonathan Whettingsteel
November 2021

CONTENTS

CHAPTER ONE

INTRODUCTION

It has been said the world is becoming a smaller place as technology advances. I would say this is true, but not just because of technological advances, which allow us to communicate with anyone anywhere in the world instantaneously, but also as world travel becomes more accessible and more affordable.

Unfortunately a prime example of how easy world travel has become was shown by how quickly the COVID-19 virus spread across the world. This showed there are no such things as distant places or boarders. The world is a smaller place than it used to be.

At the time of writing the results from the 2021 census are not yet available, but the results from the last census in 2011 showed the UK to be an increasingly culturally diverse country with 13% of the total UK population (being approximately 7.5 million people) being born overseas.

A recent article in August 2021 suggested more than 1/3rd of UK births have at least one parent born overseas, with this increasing to 80% in some parts of London.

The Office for National Statistics report; 'Families and Households in the UK: 2020' reported there were 19.4 million families in the UK. Of those, just under 8.1 million have dependent children.

With a continued increase in the number of families moving to the UK and multinational families this is also going to lead to an increase in the number of children with family links and cultural connections overseas.

In his Judgement in the 2021 case of Re: P and Another (children) (Hague Convention: Consent) [2021] All ER (D) 20 (Aug), which is covered in chapter 2 of this book, Mr. Justice Poole opened as follows;

> *"Even the most caring and able parents may struggle to protect the welfare of their children during a family breakdown. If that breakdown is then complicated by a parent wishing to move abroad, with the result that the children will live in a different country from one of their parents, the struggle can become overwhelming. International relocation almost inevitably comes at a cost and often involves a significant sacrifice for at least one of the parents."*

These remarks appropriately summarise how difficult and emotive the issue of child relocation can be.

There are a number of reasons why somebody may wish to move, both to another country and to another part of the same country. This could include wanting to be nearer to family, starting a new job, a new relationship, or just wanting a new start for a better quality of life.

If parents cannot reach an agreement about the relocation of a child the type of application that needs to be made to court for permission to move is a Specific Issue Order. The number of these applications has continued to increase each year, being 8,557 in 2018, 10,157 in 2019 and 10,887 in 2020. Between January – March in 2021 the number of Specific Issue Order applications received totaled 2,949. Based at this rate, this would suggest around 11,796 applications will be received by the end of the year.

There is no way of telling how many of these applications related to permission to remove a child from the jurisdiction as the court don't track this data (believe me, I asked!).

Prior to the COVID-19 pandemic and restriction of travel, I was seeing a notable increase in the number of clients seeking advice on removing children from the jurisdiction, both permanently and temporarily.

As the world continues to get smaller, and as travelling restrictions hopefully start to relax as we come out of the global pandemic, it is almost inevitable there will be an increase in the number of people wanting to travel with children. This will be either going to visit family whom they have not seen for some time, or relocating after this was delayed as a result of travel restrictions and / or financial uncertainty, or change in circumstances caused by the pandemic.

I expect to continue to see an increase in the number of clients seeking advice on internal and external relocation as we return to normal, and in this book hope to provide clear guidance on what to do, not just in acting for a party looking to relocate but also acting for a party who may be opposing a relocation application.

Although in this book I will refer to parents and partners / ex-partners, I would stress that the contents can refer to anyone who has care and control, or Parental Responsibility for a child. Who has care and control or Parental Responsibility of a child is however another matter for an entirely separate book in itself and the reference to parents is simply just for ease.

CHAPTER TWO

PERMISSION – DO YOU NEED IT? AND IF SO, WHO FROM?

If a parent is looking to relocate the first question they will often want to know is 'whose permission do I need?' Likewise the other parent will often ask, 'does my partner / ex-partner need my permission to move with our children?'

Although the legislation below refers to 'leave' of the court the Family Procedure Rules 2010 changed the terminology. So 'leave of the court' is now 'permission of the court' when seeking a court order granting relocation.

Where there is No Court Order Governing Child Arrangements

If there is no Section 8 order in place then a parent or party who is the primary carer for a child can move within the jurisdiction without the consent of the other parent. However, they should be aware that the other parent could make an application (including on an urgent basis) for a Prohibited Steps Order to prevent the move.

There is nothing in the Children Act 1989 to expressly prevent a parent removing a child from the Jurisdiction, however in practice if a parent removes a child without the consent of everyone who holds Parental Responsibility, this would be considered child abduction. Section 1 of the Child Abduction Act 1984 makes it an offence to take or send a child out of UK without '*the appropriate consent.*' The 'appropriate consent' is defined in Section 1(3) of this statute;

Section 1(3) Child Abduction Act 1984

In this section 'the appropriate consent', in relation to a child, means –

(a) The consent of each of the following –

- *i. The child's Mother;*
- *ii. The child's Father, if he has parental responsibility for him;*
- *iii. Any guardian of the child;*
- *iiia. Any special guardian of the child;*
- *iv. Any person named in a child arrangements order as a person with whom the child is to live;*
- *v. Any person who has custody of the child; or*

(b) The leave of the court granted under or by virtue of any provision of Part II of the Children Act 1989; or

(c) *If any person has custody of the child, the leave of the court which awarded custody to him.*

Removing a child without consent could therefore constitute the criminal offence of child abduction which carries a penalty of up to seven years' imprisonment.

The 1980 Hague Convention on Civil Aspects of International Child Abduction provides remedies for the return of a child who has been unlawfully removed or retained from the Jurisdiction to a Hague Convention country. This provides the mechanisms for the return of a child and cooperation between member states.

Therefore, in the absence of any court order, anyone who holds parental responsibility will need to be consulted before a child is removed from the jurisdiction. This could include the Local Authority where a Care Order has been granted as this would grant that Local Authority parental responsibility for the child or children named.

For internal relocation cases the need for permission is still there, but it would depend upon how far a parent is relocation and the change this would have for the child. Section 3(1) Children Act 1989 defines parental responsibility as;

> ***Section 3(1) Children Act 1989***
>
> *"all the rights, duties, powers, responsibilities and authority which by law a parent of a child has in relation to the child and his property."*

This would include which school a child attends. Therefore if a parent is looking at relocating internally and this would involve changing a child's school, then the consent of everyone holding parental responsibility would be required.

There is no set distance or exact precedent on when permission for an internal relocation is required, with this being based on each individual case, but it is sensible to seek the consent of everyone holding parental responsibility before moving as failure to do so could result in a court application and subsequent order with a parent being forced to return a child. This is addressed in more detail below.

Where there is no Child Arrangements Order in force any application for permission to relocate should be issued under Section 8 of the Children Act 1989, being a Specific Issue Order.

Where a Child Arrangements Order is in place

For an internal relocation, provided the move would not breach the terms of any existing order a parent or party who is the primary carer for a child can still move within the jurisdiction without the other parent's consent. Again though, there is a risk of that parent seeking a Prohibited Steps Order to prevent the move.

Where there is a Child Arrangements Order in force stating with whom a child shall live, any application for permission to externally relocate should be issued under Section 13 of the Children Act 1989, seeking a variation of the existing Child Arrangements Order and permission for a general or specific purpose.

Section 13(1) Children Act 1989 prohibits a child being removed from the Jurisdiction without the written consent order of everyone who holds Parental Responsibility or an order of the court. However this applies only where a Child Arrangements Order has been made for a child to 'live with' a party. Subsection 13(2) also permits the removal for a period of up to a month by a party where a Child Arrangements 'Live With' Order has been made in their favour.

There is no limit on the number of temporary removals for less than a month and if the other party wants to set a limit this would require an order of the court and a condition being attached to any order.

Section 13 does not apply for internal relocations and any applications for internal relocation will be under Section 8 Children Act 1989, irrespective of whether a Child Arrangements Order is in force.

Section 13(2) Children Act 1989

Change of child's name or removal from jurisdiction.

(1) Where a child arrangements order to which subsection (4) applies is in force with respect to a child, no person may—

(a) cause the child to be known by a new surname; or

(b) remove him from the United Kingdom;

without either the written consent of every person who has parental responsibility for the child or the leave of the court.

(2) Subsection (1)(b) does not prevent the removal of a child, for a period of less than one month, by a person named in the child arrangements order as a person with whom the child is to live.

(3) In making a child arrangements order to which subsection (4) applies, the court may grant the leave required by subsection (1)(b), either generally or for specified purposes.

(4) This subsection applies to a child arrangements order if the arrangements regulated by the order consist of, or include, arrangements which relate to either or both of the following—

(a) with whom the child concerned is to live, and

(b) when the child is to live with any person.

The removal of a child without consent and the requirement for consent is contained in Section 1(4) Child Abduction Act 1984 which states that an offence of child abduction is not committed where;

Section 1(4) Child Abduction Act 1989

A person does not commit an offence under this section by taking or sending a child out of the United Kingdom without obtaining the appropriate consent if; –

(a) He is the person named in a child arrangements order as a person with whom the child is to live and he takes or sends the child out of the United Kingdom for a period of less than one month; or

(b) He is a special guardian of the child and he takes or sends the child out of the United Kingdom for a period of less than three months

If a special guardianship order is in force then the period a child can be removed without consent is extended to three months.

Under Section 33 of the Children Act a Local Authority who has a care order in their favour can also remove a child from the jurisdiction for a period of up to one month without consent.

It is important to ensure that the removal of a child would not breach any court orders in place. For example, if the removal would mean a child does not have the court ordered contact then this would require the consent of the other party due to have contact or variation of the court order otherwise this would constitute a breach of a Child Arrangements Order. This is something that is often overlooked by a parent who has a child arrangements 'live with' order. The requirement to provide the child for contact would override the right to be able to remove the child for up to one month.

If removing a child in excess of these periods then it is necessary to seek the appropriate consent as set out above.

> *It should also be noted that Section 1(5) Child Abduction Act 1989 states an offence is not committed where;*
>
> 1. *The removing party believes;*
>   a. *The other person consented; or*
>   b. *Would consent if they were aware of all of the relevant circumstances; or*
>
> 2. *Has taken all reasonable steps to communicate with the other person but has been unable to do so; or*
>
> 3. *The other person has unreasonably refused to consent.*

The refusal to consent cannot be overridden without a court order if the person refusing to consent is named in a Child Arrangements Order as a person with whom the child lives, is a Special Guardian, has custody of the child, or the removal of the child would be a breach of a court order. A practical example of this would be if the removal of the child would mean the child was not provided for court ordered contact (Section 5A Child Abduction Act 1989).

How to prove consent

As noted above, Section 13(1) prohibits the removal of a child without the *written* consent of everyone who holds parental responsibility. There is no definition as to what format the written consent needs to take.

Where there is no Child Arrangements 'Live With' Order in force, there is no legal requirement for consent to be provided in writing. However, it is sensible and much safer to do so. This prevents any dispute arising in future as to whether or not consent has been given.

For internal relocation there is no express requirement that consent needs to be in writing. However, again it would be sensible and good practice to do so.

There is no definitive statutory guidance as to how a parent would provide consent and what this 'consent' should look like with much of the guidance coming from case law.

The meaning of consent and the form that it should take was considered by Ward LJ in the case of Re P-J (Children) (removal outside jurisdiction: abduction) [2009] All ER (D) 242 (Jun). He noted at paragraph 44 of his Judgement that there is '*surprisingly little authority on what constitutes sufficient consent.*' Reference was made to Hale J, as she was at the time considering this issue in the case of Re K (Abduction: Consent) [1997] 2 FLR 212. She had to weigh up the two conflicting views of Holman JJ and Wall J in the case of Re: W (Abduction: Procedure) [1995] 1 FLR 878. Holman J stated consent did not need to be evidenced in writing;

> *". . . parents do not necessarily expect to reduce their agreements and understandings about their children into writing, even at a time of marital breakdown. What matters is that consent is 'established'. The means of proof will vary."*

Holman JJ did not agree with this, stating;

> *"It follows, in my judgment, that where a parent seeks to argue the Article 13(a) 'consent' defence under the Hague Convention, the*

> *evidence for establishing consent needs to be clear and compelling. In normal circumstances, such consent will need to be in writing or at the very least evidenced by documentary evidence. Moreover, unlike acquiescence, I find it difficult to conceive of circumstances in which consent could be passive: there must in my judgment be clear and compelling evidence of a positive consent to the removal of the child from the jurisdiction of his habitual residence."*

Hale J gave wording which now appears to be accepted that consent must be 'unequivocal'. Giving judgement in the above case of Re: K she stated;

> *"It is obvious that consent must be real. It must be positive and it must be unequivocal. But that is a separate issue from the nature of the evidence required to establish it. There will be circumstances in which the court can be satisfied that such consent has been given even though it has not been given in writing. It stands to reason, however, that most people who wish to retain or remove a child would be well advised to get written consent before they do so to place the matter beyond argument. There may also be circumstances in which it can be inferred from conduct."*

The comments of Ward LJ were considered by Poole J in Re P and another (children) (Hague Convention: consent) [2021] EWHC 2184 (Fam).

In paragraph 39 of the Judgement Poole J endorsed the comments in Re P-J of Ward LJ;

> *"As Ward LJ noted, for consent to be valid it must be unequivocal and informed, and it must have been given prior to the removal. Consent obtained by fraud will not be considered valid."*

Re P-J also considered how much in advance of removal consent must be given. It was confirmed consent does not need to be instantaneously at the time, and consent can be given that removal will take place in the future, or even at '*an indefinite date*' (judgement paragraph 46).

Paragraph 48 of the Judgement of Ward LJ provides helpful guidance on the issue of consent;

> *(1) Consent to the removal of the child must be clear and unequivocal.*
>
> *(2) Consent can be given to the removal at some future but unspecified time or upon the happening of some future event.*
>
> *(3) Such advance consent must, however, still be operative and in force at the time of the actual removal.*

Re: D (a child: Habitual Residence: Consent and Acquiescence) [2015] All ER (D) 158 (Jun) [2015] EWHC 1562 (Fam) confirmed the above comments of Ward LJ

These comments were also referenced and confirmed in some of the most recent cases to look at consent.

In A v B [2021] All ER (D) 03 (Jul) [2021] EWHC 1716 (Fam) consideration was given on consent. The parents had agreed an order by consent not to remove the child from the jurisdiction. There was no end date to this period. This case also provides helpful guidance on port alerts to prevent a removal. This confirmed for a port alert to be made there needed to be a 'real and imminent' risk of removal. This confirmed a port alert should also only last for 28 days in the first instance, and that any application should be made to the family court, not the High Court.

The case of Re: P and another (children) (Hague Convention: Consent) [2021] EWHC 2184 (Fam) [2021] All ER (D) 20 (Aug). This case concerned a Father's application under the Hague Convention (more on that in Chapter 6) for the return of his two children who were removed from the United States to the UK by their Mother. The Father's case was that his consent had been obtained by the Mother using dishonest means.

There were two children from a marriage, aged 11 and 12 at the time of the Judgement. The parties resided in America and the Mother was offered a temporary three year employment contract in England as an IT manager. The Father initially opposed the move and there were a number of email exchanges between the parents in July 2020. It was accepted that the Father did agree to the Mother and children moving to England after a number of emails, and in late July the parties attended before a notary and signed a written agreement stating;

"[The Father] consents to both minors [the children] residing and travelling abroad with their Mother..... for employment and / or leisure purposes. As such [the Mother] will assume primary physical custody on 01 august 2020 of both minor children."

The parents also signed a separation and custody agreement confirming joint legal custody of the children, and that the children would live primarily with the Mother.

The Father then started making attempts to sell the family home in America. He visited the children in the UK in November 2020 until January 2021.

In March 2021 the Father made an application to the High Court for a without notice location order (despite at that time being in England and in the same town as to where the Mother and children were living).

The Mother's contract of employment was with the US Government, and as such when being stationed abroad she was entitled to a package of benefits. It was the Father's position that his consent to the removal of the children was given on the basis the Mother would have him listed as a dependent upon her orders by January 2021. This would allow him to also benefit from the Mother's employment package and move to England to join the Mother and children. The Mother sent an email after the move to England saying that as the couple had separated her employer would not include the Father as a dependent. The Father's case was that he had been tricked in to giving his consent.

There were a number of points for the court to wrestle with, including determining whether the Hague Convention applied, the habitual residence of the children, whether the Mother had unlawfully retained the children and whether the children were at risk if the court ordered their return. This is a useful case to refer to for a commentary on the current position on return cases.

In determining whether consent had been given Mr. Justice Poole had to consider whether the Father's consent was *"unequivocal and informed or was it obtained by duplicitous means or misinformation and therefore vitiated?"* (paragraph 4 of the Judgement). If addressing the court on consent *"unequivocal and informed"* are the key words.

The burden of proof for determining whether consent has been given rests on the person relying on it. So in short it, was for the Mother to prove the Father had consent, not for him to prove that he hadn't. However when it came to showing the children had been unlawfully retained, the burden of proof fell on the Father.

Upon analysing the documents the Judge was satisfied there was nothing recorded to state the Father's consent was conditional upon being named as a dependent by January 2021. Likewise, the Judge stated that there was nothing in the written exchanges between the parents where the Father alleged trickery or dishonesty by the Mother.

In paragraph 54 of the Judgement it was stated:

> *"When considering all the evidence in this case I remind myself that emails and written messaging have to be considered in the context of a marriage breakdown, heightened feelings, changing information, and many oral conversations that are not recorded. It would be wrong to approach the communications between the parties as if analysing the terms of a commercial contract. This is a family case. I have regard to the whole of the evidence and the circumstances of the time. Some statements are made in the heat of the moment, when in a rush or when tempers are raised, others are more considered. Not all emails or messages should be given equal weight. Nor should the court approach the statements and agreements as though this were a contract law case."*

This may be a useful point to raise if disputing that the agreement between the parties is more than what has been recorded in writing or that something was said in the heat of the moment.

The key points to take from this Judgement are that the court gave weighting to written communications between the parties, as well as the separation agreement and travel consent form. If you are looking at evidencing consent, although formal documents are not essential, they would certainly be sensible and would carry weighting with the court, and if conditions are given on consent these should be confirmed in writing and prior to removal.

Removal without consent

If a child is removed from the jurisdiction without consent, this would constitute a child abduction. The law and process around this is too much to do justice to in this section and is a separate book in itself.

If a child has been removed and relocated within the jurisdiction without the appropriate consent then the remedy is for the parent to issue an urgent application to the court for a Section 8 Children Act Order. A Specific Issue Order is a must, seeking the return of the children, along with a Prohibited Steps Order Preventing the further removal. It is however also worth considering what measures are required to prevent a further removal. This could include the surrender of a child and / or Parent's passport to the court or solicitors under a Specific Issue Order, a Prohibited Steps Order to prevent the children being removed from a parent's care if the removal followed an unlawful retention and a Child Arrangements Order. The remedies required will depend on the circumstances and risks in each case.

Likewise, if a parent believes there is a genuine risk of a child being removed from the jurisdiction, or relocated within the jurisdiction without their consent then they should apply for a Prohibited Steps Order. Prevention of removal is often the best remedy rather than seeking a return following removal.

If a child has been removed or retained outside of the Jurisdiction then an application can be made under the 1980 Hague Convention. Article 3 outlines what is considered an unlawful removal and retention and Article 8 the provisions for the return of the children. If consent is being argued by the removing parent this would be considered under Article 13 of the convention.

There is little case law on consent for internal relocation cases, however good practice would be to apply similar procedures to external relocation cases and indeed the guidance from the case of Re: C (A child) (Internal relocation) [2015] EWCA 1305 suggests that there was no distinction between internal and external relocation cases.

CHAPTER THREE

PRE-PROCEEDINGS

The first step should be to look at obtaining the consent of everyone who holds Parental Responsibility for the children. As noted in chapter 2, consent must be unequivocal, informed and given before the removal of the child(ren). If consent is given this should be recorded in a written document, such as a separation agreement if parties have recently separated or a travel consent. It is sensible to check with the country that a child will be travelling too as some countries, such as South Africa have specific forms that are required.

If an agreement cannot be reached and there is a dispute over the removal of the children then an application to the court is likely to be needed. The relocation of a child is often something that does require the court's determination as unlike contact arrangements, it is not something where a compromise can be achieved as the child will either remain in the jurisdiction or leave.

Section 10(1) of the Children and Families Act 2014 makes it a mandatory requirement for a party to attend a Family Mediation Information and Assessment Meeting (MIAM) before a court application can be issued. Rule 3.8 of the Family Procedure Rules 2010 outlines the circumstances where an exemption to attend a MIAM may apply. This includes;

1. *Where there is evidence of domestic abuse;*

2. *Where there are child protection concerns;*

3. *Urgency – Where a delay in issuing a court application would result in;*

    a. *A risk to the life, liberty or physical safety of the prospective applicant or his or her family home;*

b. *A risk of harm to a child;*

c. *A risk of unlawful removal of a child from the UK or a risk of unlawful retention of a child who is outside of England and Wales*

d. *A significant miscarriage of justice;*

e. *Unreasonable hardship;*

f. *Irretrievable problems in dealing with the dispute;*

g. *A significant risk that in the period required to arrange and attend a MIAM a court application may be made in another state where a valid claim on jurisdiction would exist and the court in the other state may be seised of the dispute before the courts of England and Wales.*

4. *The applicant attended a MIAM or other form of dispute resolution in the four months prior to issuing the application and the application relates to the same dispute;*

5. *The application is being made in existing proceedings which are continuing and a MIAM exemption applied to those proceedings;*

6. *One or more of the parties is subject to a disability which prevents their attendance at a MIAM unless appropriate facilities can be offered by the mediator and no such facilities can be offered by a mediator within fifteen miles of the party;*

7. *One or more of the parties is in prison or subject to a licence or conditions which prevents their attendance at a MIAM;*

8. *No mediators are available within fifteen miles;*

9. *The mediator has been the matter as unsuitable for mediation*

It is difficult to envisage a situation whereby an exemption would apply for urgency by the party seeking the removal of the child, however it is possible that if one parent believes the other may be imminently removing the child from the jurisdiction without consent an exemption my apply under urgency to prevent their removal.

If parties are going through Children Act proceedings, such as for a Child Arrangements Order and during these proceedings one parent decides to relocate with the children, or even remove them from the jurisdiction for a holiday then this would be covered as an exemption under points 4 or 5 above.

If an agreement cannot be reached at mediation, which is often the case due to the nature of the dispute, if the matter is deemed unsuitable, or an exemption applies then the matter is likely to require the determination of the court.

If the matter is going to proceed to court then any party seeking permission to relocate will be expected to set out a clear plan. Whilst a non-exhaustive list there are a number of things a client should be advised to consider;

- Why they want to relocate? – is this for their benefit, the child's benefit or to obstruct the relationship with the other parent;
- The reason behind the move? – is this for employment, a new relationship, returning to a home country, moving nearer to family, a change in lifestyle or better standard of living;
- Where will they and the child(ren) be living? – look at property particulars, how will they fund any purchase / rent / mortgage;
- Where will they work? – consider getting a letter confirming a job offer if applicable;
- What income will the party have? How will they afford to meet their outgoings? Are they moving to a cheaper or more expensive area? Will any move impact upon their income?
- Local facilities – where is the nearest dentist, GP, school and are there places available? For schools look at local OFSTED or other such equivalent reports;

- What support will be available? – such as family or friends who live in the area;

- What contact will take place with the remaining parent / party? How will this be managed, including direct and indirect contact, including travel arrangements;

- Will any documentation or permissions be required from any jurisdiction to which they are moving? What would their immigration status be? Would this be temporary or permanent?;

- Will a mirrored order be required or other arrangements to make any order binding in another jurisdiction?;

- What impact would it have on the parent seeking to relocate if the application was refused?

Look at obtaining evidence for any of the above, such as property particulars, letters from employers, school reports, evidence of places at schools, GP surgeries, dentists, etc. For internal relocations, a route planner should also be considered showing the distance between the parents and travel time if permission to relocate was granted. For external relocations look at obtaining evidence of travel availability showing the time and cost of flights or other travel options. It is important a parent is able to demonstrate how they will continue to promote contact and the relationship between the remaining parent if permission is granted.

As above, this is a non-exhaustive list. The court will take a holistic approach, looking at the full circumstances, but the above list should provide helpful guidance for things for a client to consider before applying to relocate and will demonstrate that this is a well thought out plan. Ultimately the least amount of uncertainty that a parent can provide as to how life would be after relocating the better.

If advising a parent / party who is opposing an application to relocate then the above should also be considered and also consideration given to;

- The current level of contact they have with the child(ren) and what impact would relocation have on this;

- What would the practical difficulties be in contact after relocation;

- Are there any issues with the resources available in the proposed relocation area, again they may wish to look at school reports and availability of spaces at local schools, GPs, dentists, etc;

- Are the children involved in any clubs or do they have any hobbies or interests? Would these be able to continue if the children were to relocate?;

- What are the child(ren)'s wishes and feelings regarding the proposed move? It is also important to consider whether they fully appreciate the impact of a permanent move. It is common that where children have been on holiday to an area they may have positive associations of a location, but may not appreciate that it would be a different reality to move and live there permanently;

- What would the impact upon the remaining parent be if the child(ren) were to relocate?

Again this is a non-exhaustive list. If the matter goes to court parties are likely to be directed to file statements addressing the above but it is sensible to consider obtaining this information from a client, along with any supporting evidence before an application is made.

CHAPTER FOUR

INTERNAL RELOCATION

a. What is 'Internal' Relocation?

An internal relocation would be a move within the United Kingdom. This would include a move outside of England and Wales to Scotland or Northern Ireland. This is as set out in Section 13(1)(b) Children Act 1989 which prohibits a removal from the UK where a Child Arrangements Order is in force.

In the case of Re H (Children) (Residence Order: Condition) [2001] 2 FLR 1277 Thorpe LJ and Astill J were required to consider whether a proposed relocation to Northern Ireland constituted an external or internal relocation. The court held, when considering Section 13(1)(b) Children Act 1989 that any move within the UK would be considered an internal relocation, this included both Scotland and Northern Ireland.

Re T (a child) [2001] EWCA Civ 1067 confirmed that where a child arrangements order is in force for where the child lives an application for removal from England and Wales to Scotland does not require an application for permission to remove from the jurisdiction, as this falls within the UK.

Where there is no Child Arrangements or other Section 8 order in place a parent or party who is the primary carer for a child may not necessarily need to apply for permission to relocate internally. However, they should be aware that the other parent may apply for a Prohibited Steps Order to prevent the move.

In circumstances where there is a Child Arrangements Order in place, unless the order expressly states otherwise, the parent or primary carer can still move within the jurisdiction without the other parent's consent as Section 13(1)(b) CA 1989 only prohibits an external relocation. They would however need to ensure that the terms of any Child Arrangements

Order are still being complied with, for example, if the child is still being provided to spend time with that parent in accordance with a Child Arrangements Order.

On 24th July 2018 the then President of the Family Division, Sir James Munby and head of the Scottish Judiciary, Lord Carloway signed a new judicial protocol. The snappily titled, '*New Judicial Protocol for Children's Cases in Scotland, and England and Wales.*' The guidance itself totals 8 pages, but is accompanied by a 100 page handbook. The purpose of the protocol is to ensure cooperation and communication between the judiciary and the courts of Scotland, and England and Wales. Practitioners should refer to this if dealing with a case involving a relocation between England and Wales, and Scotland, including the enforcement of orders in the other jurisdiction and the passing of information. The protocol applies to both private and public law children disputes. The accompanying handbook provides useful guidance on procedures, terminology and powers of both jurisdictions.

b. Opposing an Internal Relocation

If a party finds out the other parent is going to relocate with a child they should make an urgent application for a Prohibited Steps Order seeking an order preventing the child being removed from their current location. Consideration should be given to the details of the proposed move before issuing any court application to ensure there is a cost benefit. For example, if only moving a short distance that would allow the child to remain in the same locality and school / nursery then unless there is a good reason a move is unlikely to be prevented.

If there is an imminent risk of a move then this application should be made on an urgent basis, potentially without notice to the other parent, if doing so would mean they would move before the matter gets before the court.

If a parent has already moved, then a parent should seek a Specific Issue Order requiring the return of the child and a Prohibited Steps Order to prevent their further removal. This would be issued using a C100 and most likely an accompanying C1A due to the risk of child abduction. A party should also consider, if making an urgent application, submitting an accompanying statement advising why there is an urgency to the application. Although a draft order is not required it is often sensible to file this with the application too.

It is worth noting that an order prohibiting an internal relocation is only going to be made in "exceptional circumstances", such as those which applied in the case of Re: F (children) (internal relocation) [2010] EWCA Civ 1428 as summarised below.

When considering any application to prevent a removal or for the return of a child the court's primary consideration will be the welfare of the child. The court will also apply the welfare checklist as set out in Section 1(3) Children Act 1989 below. The court will often want to maintain the status quo until being able to consider all evidence and make a final decision.

Any emergency order will not be indicative of the court's final decision, and this simply maintains the status quo and prevents any change in circumstances until the court are able to make a fully informed and final decision.

If a Child Arrangements Order is made then Section 11(7) Children Act 1989 gives the court the power to attach any conditions to an order, although if specifically prohibiting the relocation of a child this should be under a separate section 8 Prohibited Steps Order rather than a condition attached to a Child Arrangements Order.

Consideration should also be given to attaching a penal notice to any prohibition to relocate meaning there would be a greater consequence for any breach, making it a criminal offence.

c. Making an Application for Internal Relocation

Where there is no Child Arrangements Order in force

If there is no Child Arrangements Order in force any application for permission to relocate should be issued under Section 8 Children Act 1989, seeking a Specific Issue Order for permission to relocate. It would also be sensible at the same time to issue an application for a Children Arrangements 'live with' Order. This would be issued on a C100, along with potentially a C1A if a parent is raising allegations of harm or a risk of abduction.

Following issue of a court application the same procedure and guidance would be followed for both applications where a Child Arrangements Order is and is not in place.

Where there is a Child Arrangements Order in force

Section 13(1)(b) prohibits the removal of a child from the UK where there is a Child Arrangements Order in force, however this does not prohibit an internal move within the UK. The other parent would therefore need to make an application for a Prohibited Steps Order to prevent a removal taking place as outlined above.

If a Child Arrangements Order is in force the parent seeking to relocate externally should issue an application under Section 13 Children Act 1989. This would be issued on a C1 for a new application or a C2 if being made within existing proceedings. This would be an application seeking to either vary an existing Child Arrangements Order if this contains a restriction preventing removal, or for permission to relocate if the order does not contain any restrictions.

For internal relocations this is under Section 8 of the Children Act only as Section 13 does not apply for internal relocations. This should be made on a C100 for new applications and on a C2 for applications within existing proceedings.

The power to impose restrictions on a Child Arrangements or other Section 8 Order is contained in Section 11(7) Children Act 1989.

Section 13(3) Children Act 1989 gives the court the power to grant permission for the removal of the child for specified purposes.

d. Returning a Child Unilaterally Removed Internally

When seeking an application to the court it is important to identify whether the application is for an internal child abduction or permission to relocate following a unilateral removal. An internal child abduction was considered in Re: R, where it was confirmed internal and external abduction cases should not be applied using the same guidance. By contrast the case of AH v DT [2017] resulted from a Mother unilaterally removing a child internally, but the court confirmed the decision of Re: C, in that internal and external relocation cases should apply the same approach and criteria.

The case of Re: R (a child) (domestic abduction) [2016] EWCA Civ 1016 considered an application for internal child abduction, with the court finding there was a distinction between the guidance for internal and external abduction cases.

Re: R (a child) (domestic abduction) [2016] EWCA Civ 1016

This case concerned an application by the Father seeking the return of his one year-old who had been removed by the Mother from Kent to what is described throughout the Judgement as the 'North East' where her family lived. The Mother accepted she moved with the child without obtaining the Father's consent or knowledge. She made a number of allegations of domestic abuse against the Father and obtained a without notice Prohibited Steps order, preventing him from removing the child from her care. The Father issued a cross application seeking the immediate return of the child to Kent. The Father's case was that following the judgement and guidance of the case of Re C the court should apply the same law for internal and external relocations and removal, ordering the return of the child and resumption of the status quo pending any determination where a removal has taken place unilaterally.

The Father's application was refused in the first instance and his appeal was also unsuccessful. The court drew a distinction between relocation and abduction cases, stating that although the approach for internal and external relocation cases was the same there was a distinction with abduction cases. The court found that Re: C sought to clarify that the list from the case of Payne v Payne was guidance, not a determinative list; effectively limiting the impact of Payne and not setting a new principle that internal and external abduction cases should be subject to the same criteria.

This can be distinguished from the case of AH v DT where the Mother was seeking permission to relocate with the child internally to Northern Ireland.

AH v DT [2017] EWHC 36 (Fam)

The Mother unilaterally removed the party's child to Northern Ireland. The Father issued an application seeking their return which was granted in the first instance. The Mother made allegations of abuse against the Father and after hearing evidence the court found that the alleged abuse had not occurred. The Mother opposed the application requiring her to return to England stating the child was now settled in Northern Ireland. The Judge in the first instance applied the guidance from Re: C, requiring internal and external relocation cases to be treated the same and upon application of the guidance ordered the Mother to return the child to England. The Mother sought to appeal the decision preparing her own skeleton argument and citing 8 different grounds, including that the Judge had failed to make the child's welfare their paramount consideration, gave priority to the Father's convenience over the best interests of the child, and did not take in to consideration that the child was settled and the impact that a return would have upon her.

In a supplemental skeleton argument filed on behalf of the Mother, her counsel argued the Judge had failed to apply the welfare principle in a 'holistic, global or comparative manner,' focusing on the Payne blueprint over the guidance of Re: C.

Permission to appeal was refused by Baker J

In giving Judgement Baker J applied and confirmed the decision of Re C; that the court should apply the same principles in external and internal relocation cases and that the child's welfare was the court's paramount consideration. It was held the decision of the Judge in the first instance was within his discretion and the guidance had been correctly applied.

e. Key Legislation

When presenting a case, either seeking or opposing an application to relocate, key consideration should be given to Section 1(1) Children Act 1989 which states that when the court are determining any question about a child, (which would include an application to relocate) 'the child's welfare shall be the court's paramount consideration'. It is well established that the welfare of the child is the overriding guidance the court should apply.

Section 1(3) – Contains 'The Welfare Checklist' that the court should apply when making decisions about a child, being;

> *(a) the ascertainable wishes and feelings of the child concerned (considered in the light of his age and understanding);*
>
> *(b) his physical, emotional and educational needs;*
>
> *(c) the likely effect on him of any change in his circumstances;*
>
> *(d) his age, sex, background and any characteristics of his which the court considers relevant;*
>
> *(e) any harm which he has suffered or is at risk of suffering;*

(f) how capable each of his parents, and any other person in relation to whom the court considers the question to be relevant, is of meeting his needs;

(g) the range of powers available to the court under this Act in the proceedings in question.

When making decisions, both in relation to internal and external relocation, the court need to consider Article 8 of the European Convention on Human Rights. Irrespective of the court's decision there will likely be an impact upon one party's right to a family life, either the remaining parent if permission to relocate is granted, or the other parent if permission is refused. When deciding matters the court will therefore need to give consideration to Article 8 of the Human Rights Act.

f. Case Law

There are limited reported cases on internal / domestic relocation, and although some of the cases below relate to applications for external relocation they provide useful guidance that does apply in internal relocation applications too.

Re: C is the current key case and guidance on the approach the court should take on internal relocation cases and has been considered and clarified in the case of Re: K.

Re: C (A child) (Internal relocation) [2015] EWCA Civ 1305

This confirms there is no difference in the criteria and factors applied in internal and external relocation cases, and the court need to consider a 'holistic approach' balancing the full circumstances and relevant factors. Ultimately, the only test that must be applied is that the welfare of the child is the court's paramount consideration (Section 1(1) Children Act 1989).

This was an application by a Mother to relocate from London to Cumbria with the party's ten year-old child. The child spent two nights a week and every other weekend with the Father, who opposed the application to relocate.

In their Section 7 report CAFCASS said that although this was a finely balance matter, it was not in the child's best interests to move. It was however acknowledged that the child had expressed a desire to move to Cumbria, and that following any move the strong relationship with the Father was likely to be maintained. In the first instance the Recorder went against the CAFCASS recommendations and permitted the Mother's application to relocate. In reaching this decision the Recorder applied the guidance from the case of Payne v Payne (*see chapter 5 on external relocations*).

An appeal was issued by the Father on the grounds the Recorder had made an error in focusing solely on the guidance from the case of Payne v Payne, as well as treating the Mother as the child's primary carer which did not reflect the actual time spent with each parent, as well as placing too much emphasis on the impact on the Mother if the application was refused.

When before the Court of Appeal, it was considered whether the general principles that should be applied to internal relocation cases should be differentiated from external relocation applications. This also considered whether there was a rule that an application for an internal move should only be refused as the exception.

In giving their judgement the Court of Appeal held there was no difference in the approach between internal and external relocation cases. There was no presumption in favour of the applicant seeking to relocate, and it was not necessary for the opposing parent to establish exceptional circumstances. The court held the only test was what is in the best interests of the child and their welfare. In determining this, the court should apply a holistic approach and balance all of the relevant factors. Consideration should be given to the Section 1(7) Children Act 1989 Welfare Checklist and the Payne guidance, the latter forming guidance only, not a strict criteria. The factors for the court to consider will differ from case to case depending on the circumstances of each case, family and child(ren)

Re: K (a child) (international relocation: appeal against judge's finds of fact) [2016] EWCA Civ 931 [2016] All ER (D) 30

This case considered the judgement of Re: C above and provided further clarification on the interpretation of the judgement.

The proceedings related to the party's 10 year-old daughter. The Mother came from the Republic of Ireland, and the Father from England. Following their separation the Mother initially remained in England with the child having regular contact with her Father.

The Mother applied for permission to permanently relocate to the Republic of Ireland with the child. The Father opposed this and during the course of the proceedings the Mother made three allegations of incidents that she alleged occurred between the child and the child's Father, where the Father acted in a violent, angry or otherwise inappropriate way towards the child.

The Judge found that the Mother had not fabricated the incidents, nor encouraged the child to make them, however with two of the three alleged incidents it was held there was insufficient evidence to determine they had occurred. In respect of the third incident the Judge held that this had occurred.

The Judge applied the welfare checklist, including the child's wishes and feelings and determined the child did want to move to the Republic of Ireland, and also enjoyed spending time with her Father. It was determined the child's wishes and feelings could be met in either jurisdiction. The Judge felt that if permission to relocate was refused, this would negatively impact upon the Mother which too would be detrimental to the child. The Judge further stated that there were concerns. The Father was trying to control the Mother by preventing her moving and should this continue this too would adversely impact upon the child. It was stated the relationship between the child and her Father could still continue.

An appeal was submitted by the Father on three grounds;

i) The Judge erred in her approach to the allegations that he had acted in an angry, violent or otherwise inappropriate way. This was on the basis the Judge determined it was necessary to make findings but then did not make clear and definite conclusions, leaving insufficient information upon which to base her decision;

ii) Not properly considering the Father's submissions that the Mother is likely to make further allegations of harm to the child and impede his relationship in the future;

iii) Failing to undertake a 'sophisticated, comparative, holistic analysis; or carrying out a 'proportionality assessment' as required under the authority of Re: C.

The Father's appeal was dismissed on the following grounds;

i) The Judge had made a conclusion about whether or not the alleged incidents had taken place on the balance or probability;

ii) As the Judge found the Mother had not fabricated the allegations or made the child make them, it was expected the Judge would decline to determine the Mother would make further allegations in the future;

iii) Although it was confirmed the Judge had given greater consideration and scrutiny to the Mother's proposals, this did not mean the Father's proposals and position had been ignored. This was simply as the proposals being made by the Mother were new and by contrast the Father's position was known, in that he was opposing the move on the grounds this would impact upon his relationship with the child. The Judge's approach was appropriate, and based on the welfare of the child.

Providing clarification on the Judgement of Re: C it was held that Re: C did not endorse a separate consideration of the orders being proposed by the parents as a whole, but that Re: C intended that when determining the best interests of the child this would involve the court given careful consideration of a number of factors independently, including the parents' wishes, their right to a family life under Article 8 of the Human Rights Act, and the impact of the court's decision on the parents and child.

Payne v Payne [2001] 1 FLR 1052

This case is addressed in more detail in the next chapter on external relocation, however the above case of Re: C (A child) (internal relocation) confirmed that the checklist from the case of Payne provides a 'blueprint' for internal and external relocation cases, but these are not an exhaustive and prescriptive list and the court can attach whatever weighting they deem appropriate to these points, as well as having discretion as to which of the points they consider.

Nazarenko v Russia (Application No. 39438/13 [2015] 2 FLR 728

The circumstances of this case are rather unique but this case does provide some useful guidance on the interpretation of Article 8 of the European Convention of Human Rights in relocation cases.

The Mother and Father were Russian nationals and had one daughter from their marriage, who was born in in 2007. The parties separated in 2010 and shared care of the child. The Father refused to return the child to the care of the Mother after discovering bruising on her, which he suspected was caused by the Mother's new partner. Both parents issued cross applications for the child to reside with them. Despite the fact that the child had spent the last year with the Father following his refusal to return. The court found the parents had shared equal care of the child's upbringing. Taking in to consideration a number of factors, including the age and sex of the child, the court directed it was preferable she reside with her Mother. The Father refused to return the child to the Mother and so she abducted the child from the Father's care.

During proceedings DNA testing was undertaken which revealed that the Father was in fact not the biological Father of the child. Following this development the court dismissed the Father's application for residence, as well as removing his name from the child's birth certificate and permitting the child's name to be changed. This was upheld by the Supreme Court, however the Father applied to the European Court of Human Rights, suggesting he was not made aware of the Supreme Court hearing.

The Father's application was that the termination of his paternity was a breach of Article 8 of the Human Rights Act – his right to a family life.

The European Court of Human Rights upheld the Father's application, finding there had been a breach of Article 8.

The court found that where a family tie had been established, the state must act in a manner to enable that tie to be maintained. It held that, although not the biological Father, a relationship of Father and daughter had been created as they had a close emotional bond and believed themselves to be Father and daughter for a number of years. This amounted to family life as per the interpretation of Article 8 of the Human Rights Act.

The point to take from this unusual set of circumstances is that it is not necessary for there to be a biological connection for a family life to have been created for the purposes of Article 8 of the Human Rights Act.

Re: E (Residence: Imposition of Conditions) [1997] 2 FLR 638

The Mother was seeking permission to relocate internally with the party's two children. This was alongside contested proceedings, with both parents also seeking the children reside with them. The judge in the First Instance determined that the issue of with whom the children should live, be determined separately from where they should live. Although the court determined the children should reside with the Mother this did not mean permission should be granted for her to relocate, and in fact the Judge in the first instance imposed a condition under Section 11(7) of the Children Act 1989 requiring the children to reside at a specified address unless the Father agreed otherwise. This was appealed by the Mother.

The Mother's appeal was successful. The Court of Appeal determined that although the court had the power to impose a condition requiring children to reside at a specified address this should only be ordered in 'exceptional cases.' It was also held that the issue of where the children should live should be considered as a relevant factor when determining with whom the children should live, not as a separate issue. If both parents are seeking the children reside with them and one parent is seeking to move with the children, then where it is proposed the children will be living should be considered alongside that parent's full proposals.

Re: S (a child) (residence order: condition) [2001] All ER (D) 159 (May) [2002] EWCA Civ 1795

This case considered the guidance of Re: E and what constituted an 'exceptional case' so as to justify the making of conditions under Section 11(7) of the Children Act 1989 imposing conditions on where a parent should reside. Following separation the parties agreed that the child should reside with the Mother but spend regular time with Father and his extended family.

The Mother had formed a new relationship and her partner was renovating a property in Cornwall to make it suitable for the child's additional medical needs. Upon hearing of this, and the Mother's plan to relocate with the child to Cornwall from where the family lived in South London, the Father made a number of court applications, including seeking a Prohibited Steps Order preventing the Mother from moving with the child.

The child had Down's Syndrome and a congenital heart and lung defect, as well as moderate learning difficulties. The child had a limited life expectancy, and was not expected to live beyond the age of 20. During proceedings the Judge heard evidence from an expert in the educational needs of children with learning disorders. The expert stated the child would find it difficult to adjust to the reduced contact with her Father that would result should they relocate to Cornwall.

The court made an order that the child reside with the Mother and imposed conditions prohibiting her from relocating. The Mother appealed, stating the facts did not satisfy being an 'exceptional case.'

The Mother's appeal was allowed with the Court of Appeal finding that the court of first instance were not to impose conditions to try and create an ideal beyond what the parties were putting forward as their proposal. The intention of the statute was to impose restrictions where the primary carer was seeking to remove the child from the jurisdiction.

The court held it was important to not impose restrictions on the primary carer's freedom to choose their preferred family life and location for two reasons;

> *"The first is that often the notion of such restrictions are simply contrary to good sense; and*
>
> *Secondly, because the imposition of restrictions is likely to have an adverse effect on the welfare of the children indirectly through the emotional and psychological disturbance caused to the primary carer by denial of the freedom to exercise reasonable choice"* (Paragraph 16 of the judgement of Lord Justice Thorpe).

In paragraph 17 of his judgement Thorpe LJ quoted Butler-Sloss LJ in the above case of Re: E;

> *"In my view the principles set out in a long line of authorities relating to leave to remove permanently from the jurisdiction have no application to conditions proposed under S 11(7)."*

Continuing his judgement at paragraph 18 he stated;

> *"With that I am in complete agreement in the sense that it is not ordinarily necessary for primary career who seek to make a local move to have to clear the various hurdles that confront an application for permission to move out of the United Kingdom. In such cases the applicant has to demonstrate that he or she has made a thorough research and exploration of the circumstances and conditions in the*

> *country to which he or she aspires to relocate and that the proposals are practical and reasonable. Such an applicant also has to meet whatever opposition there may be from the secondary carer on the front of reduction of contact or other suggested adverse consequences of relocation. Whatever tests are applied to the applicant under section 13(1)(b), they must inevitably be more stringent than the test applied to the primary carer seeking a purely local relocation."*

The imposition of conditions under Section 11(7) Children Act 1989 related solely to the removal from the jurisdiction, and should be restricted to cases where the court had direct concerns about the ability of the primary carer to achieve satisfactory standards. It was held that the judge had failed to consider the impact the Mother's feelings and aspirations would have upon the child's welfare. The appeal was granted, imposed conditions lifted and matter remitted for reconsideration to consider the educational disadvantages a relocation may have upon the child, and also the disadvantages that imposing a restriction may have upon the Mother, her partner and their 'adult freedoms.'

Re: F (children) (internal relocation) [2010] EWCA Civ 1428

The Mother was seeking a Specific Issue Order granting permission to relocate with the party's four children from the north-east of England to the Orkney Islands where the Mother's new husband / the children's step-Father had been offered a job. The Father opposed the application and three of the four children also expressed a wish that they did not wish to relocate with the fourth stating that she did wish to move. The Mother set out a contact proposal whereby the children would make seven trips per year to see their Father each taking between 9-19 hours in travel. The trips would require a change of transport and some of the return legs would require an overnight stay part way through the journey.

The Judge in the first instance determined this to be a *"truly exceptional"* case stating the proposed move came *"as close to removal from the jurisdiction as one can get,"* so as to warrant the refusal to permit an internal relocation. The decision was appealed by the Mother.

The Court of Appeal again emphasised that it would be unusual for the court to interfere with the primary carer's general right to choose where he or she would live and with whom, there could nevertheless be 'exceptional circumstances' in which conditions would have to be imposed interfering with that right in order to protect the best interest of the child and dismissed the appeal. This does however demonstrate the very high benchmark that needs to be satisfied to meet the 'exceptional circumstances' so as to justify the court refusal an internal application to relocate.

CHAPTER FIVE

EXTERNAL RELOCATION

a. What is 'external' relocation?

The guidance under Section 13(1)(b) and decision of Re: H (children) (residence order: condition) [2001] 2 FLR 1277 confirmed that an internal relocation constituted a relocation anywhere within the United Kingdom *(see chapter 4 on internal relocation)*. It therefore follows that an external relocation would be a move to anywhere outside of the United Kingdom.

When looking at the location of a proposed external relocation consideration should be given as to whether the proposed location is a Hague Convention country as this will impact upon the measures that can be put in place to enforce any order or seek a child's return. The Hague Convention can also cover child contact between member state countries. This is covered in more detail in Chapter 8.

b. Opposing / Preventing an External Relocation

Section 13(1)(b) of the Children Act 1989 prohibits the removal of a child from the United Kingdom without the written consent of every person who holds parental responsibility or the leave (now called permission) of the court. This is subject to conditions where a Child Arrangements 'Live With' Order or Special Guardianship Order is in force. Chapter 2 of this book covers the nature of permission.

If seeking to prevent a child being removed from the jurisdiction an application should be made for a Prohibited Steps Order. Where there is a concern that the child is to be removed imminently, the police should be notified and an 'all ports' warning can be issued. This will record an entry on the police national computer systems and notify officers at all ports and airports who will then prevent the children being removed from the country. Before making a port alert the police must be satisfied the danger of removal is 'real and imminent' as defined under The Child Abduction Act 1984. 'Real' is defined as not being sought merely by way of insurance and 'imminent' as within the next 24 to 48 hours. This is defined under paragraph 4.6 Practice Direction 12F of the Family Procedure Rules. For children aged 16 or 17 an all ports warning will require a court order.

The procedure and guidance for an all ports alert is set out in Part 4 of Practice Direction 12F of the Family Procedure Rules.

The case of A v B [2021] highlighted that an application for an all ports warning should be made to the family court, not the High Court and that in the first instance should last for 28 days. The application by the Father in this instance was refused as the court were not satisfied there was a 'real and imminent' threat of removal. This was on the grounds the Mother did not hold the child's passport and also as her contact was being supervised. It was therefore held to be unlikely the Mother would be able to get past the supervisor to abduct the child.

If a court application is made for a Prohibited Steps Order to prevent a removal consideration should be given to measures that can be put in place to prevent a removal and breach of the court order. This could include the surrender of a parent and / or child's passport.

c. Temporary Removal and Safeguards

If an application to relocate is temporary, even if still for a number of years then consideration should be given as to which safeguards can be put in place to ensure the return of the parent and / or child at the end of the defined period.

In Re: K (removal from jurisdiction: practice) [1999] 2 FLR 1084 it was noted that, for applications for temporary removal, the court should not rely on the parties impeccable conduct and undertakings from the parents. Particularly where removal is to a non-Hague Convention country. The court should build in as many safeguards as possible to ensure the return of the child. This could include requiring the parent to obtain a mirrored order in the country they are going to. The court will need to be sure there are mechanisms in place to enforce the order should a parent fail to return.

The court could also look at providing the remaining parent with full details of the visit, including location, duration, flight and accommodation details, contact information and seeking undertakings not to apply for duplicate passports or travel documents.

Expert evidence may also be required on the law in the other jurisdiction, particularly where a move is to be to a non-Hague Convention country.

Where an application is for a temporary removal, different factors will be applied from those which apply to applications to permanently relocate. For temporary removals there is no requirement for the court to consider the blueprint from Payne. The court will still need to apply and consider the welfare checklist, and the child's welfare being made the court's paramount consideration. The court will need to consider the specific facts of the case, for example in the case of Re: A (Temporary removal from jurisdiction) [2004] EWCA Civ 1587 the Mother was seeking permission to move to South Africa for two years for work opportunities. In making their decision the court needed to weigh up the impact upon the Mother's career should the application be refused, against the impact of the child moving to South Africa for two years, as well as factoring in what arrangements can be made to ensure continued contact and a relationship with the left behind parent.

The court need to consider what safeguards can be put in place to ensure compliance with any order, including the child being provided for any ordered contact and their return at the ordered time. The case of Re: C-W (a child) [2015] EWCA Civ 1272 [2015] All ER (D) 114 (Dec) gave useful guidance on the safeguards the court may accept. Following the breakdown of the marriage, the Father and child moved from the United States of America to the United Kingdom. The Mother issued an application under the Hague Convention for the return of the child but was unsuccessful, with the court making an order the child reside with the Father. The Mother sought an order for the child to have contact with her in Florida. This was initially refused due to concerns that the Mother may refuse to return the child. Upon issuing an appeal, the Mother offered the following safeguards;

- An American attorney would collect and hold the child's passport upon her arrival in America;
- The passport would be returned to the flight attendant at the end of the child's stay in America;
- The above two points would be confirmed to the Father;
- A 'mirror order' would be made in Florida before the child travelled. This would expressly state the child was only permitted to travel between the UK and USA and would grant the courts in Florida the power to require the child's return to the UK and Father's care without a hearing if the deadline for the child's return was not met.

The court of appeal also annexed a copy of the judgement to the order.

Based on the above safeguards the Court of Appeal granted the Mother's application, permitting the child to travel to Florida for contact.

If a temporary removal is being sought to a non-Hague Convention Country then additional safeguards and protection may be required.

The current leading guidance comes from the case of Re: R (Children: Temporary Leave To Remove From Jurisdiction) [2014] EWHC 643 (Fam) [2014] All ER (D). The Court of Appeal considered the decisions in two cases and stated the following principles will apply in an application to remove a child to a non-Hague Convention country;

- The overriding consideration for the court when deciding whether to allow a child to be taken to a non-Hague Convention country is whether the making of that order would be in the best interests of the child;

- The starting point is Section 1 Children Act 1989 – in that the child's welfare must be the court's paramount consideration and the court should have regard to each of the Section 1(3) Children Act 1989 Welfare Checklist factors;

- The court must also have regard to the European Convention of Human Rights, specifically Article 8 and the right to respect for private and family life, applying this to both the child and the parents and the orders must be proportionate and in the child's best welfare interests;

- The magnitude of the risk of breach of the order if permission is given;

- The magnitude of the consequence if a breach occurs;

- The court must be positively satisfied that the advantages to the child in visiting outweigh the risks to their welfare of any abduction / retention;

- The court must investigate what safeguards can be put in place to minimize the risk of retention and how to secure the child's return if this occurs;

- The safeguards must have a 'real and tangible' effect in the jurisdiction to which the child is travelling and being easily accessible by the party remaining in the UK;

- There is a need in most cases for the effectiveness of any safeguard to be established by competent and complete expert evidence;

- If in doubt the court should err on the side of caution and refuse to make the order;

- If the judge decides to proceed in the absence of any expert evidence very clear reasons to justify such a course of action must be given.

In the case of Re: M (a child) (temporary removal to Kurdistan) the court refused permission, permitting the Mother to temporarily remove the child for a family holiday and reunion. This was on the grounds that the risk to the child's health, safety and wellbeing in travelling to Kurdistan at that time, outweighed the benefit in visiting family. The court found the risks to the child was real and significant and there could be a real risk of physical or psychological harm, or even death and that the Mother was unable to protect the child from such risks, even if she wanted to and the Mother was not in a position to take any steps to reduce the risk to an acceptable level.

In the cases of both C v K [2014] EWHC 4125 (Fam) [2014] All ER (d) 64 (Dec) and AB v TB (Temporary removal to Jordan) [2014] EWHC 4663 (Fam) [2014] All ER (D) 252 (Dec) the court heard expert evidence on Albanian and Jordanian law respectively. Although in C v K the Mother was refused permission to take the children to Albania and in AB v TB permission was granted. The difference between the two was the court heard expert evidence on the safeguards that could be put in place and found in the case of AB v TB that the benefit to the children in visiting Jordan outweighed the risks. The Father also offered the following additional securities;

- Declarations about the children's habitual residence and the court's jurisdiction over them;

- Undertakings on oath by the Father about his commitment to return the children at the end of the designated period;

- A financial contribution of £2,500 by way of bonds;

- A further amount of money to be held by the Mother's legal representatives in Jordan to cover the costs of registering the order in Jordan

Likewise in the case of Re M and K (children) (temporary leave to remove to a non-convention country) [2016] All ER (D) 114 (Mar) the court required the Mother to provide £5,000 which would be held by the court and provided to the Father to cover his legal costs should she not return the children.

This case also affirmed the guidance from the case of Re: K (Removal from jurisdiction practice) [1999] 2 FLR 1084 that when considering an application for temporary removal the court need to consider;

- The magnitude of the risk of breach of the order if permission is given;
- The magnitude of the consequence of breach if it occurs; and
- The level of security that may be achieved by building in to the arrangements all of the available safeguards.

It should be noted that, in the case of K v K [2020] All ER (D) 123 (Dec) Mostyn J acknowledged that, where a Mother did not have the financial means to provide any security ensuring her return. This did not mean that her application should fail. The key point for the court to consider was the level of risk of the Mother breaching the order by failing to return the child.

Where there is an application to temporarily remove the child from the jurisdiction consideration should be given as to what safeguards and conditions can be put in place to ensure compliance with the order and the child's return. When deciding whether to grant permission, the court will be weighing up the benefit to the child in taking the trip against the risk of harm, both of a breach of the order and also to the safety and wellbeing of the child, with the overriding principle being that the child's welfare is the court's paramount consideration.

d. Making an Application for External Relocation

In 2001 judgement was given in the case of Payne v Payne [2001] 1 FLR 1052 which became the leading case and guidance on relocation. However since then the 'checklist' given in Payne has been made into a 'blueprint' as guidance rather than a mandatory checklist. The Payne blueprint therefore now needs to be considered alongside the judgements from the Court of Appeal in the following cases;

- K v K (children) (removal from jurisdiction) [2011] EWCA Civ 793 [2011] All ER (D) 67 (Jul),

- Re: F (a child) (permission to relocate) [2012] EWCA Civ 1364 [2013] 1 FLR 645 and

- Re: F (a child) (international relocation cases) [2015] EWCA Civ 882 [2015] All ER (D) 90 (Aug).

These all warn against overreliance on the Payne guidance.

Payne v Payne [2001] 1 FLR 1052

Following the breakdown of the marriage, the Mother applied to the court for permission to return to New Zealand, where she was originally from with the party's child. The Father opposed this, wanting the child to remain in the country with him, making his own cross application for a residence order. The court made a residence order in favour of the Mother and granted permission for her to relocate to New Zealand. The Father issued an appeal on the grounds the Judge had applied principles that gave preference to the applicant parent.

In considering the matter the Court of Appeal set out in paragraph 40 of the Judgement a list of questions to be considered in relocation cases;

(a) Is the Mother's application genuine in the sense that it is not motivated by some selfish desire to exclude the Father from the child's life?

(b) Is the Mother's application realistic, meaning founded on practical proposals, both well researched and investigated?

If the application fails either of these two tests refusal will inevitably follow

If however the application passes these tests then there must be careful consideration of the Father's opposition;

(c) *Is it motivated by genuine concern for the future of the child's welfare or is it driven by some ulterior motive?*

(d) *What would be the extent of the detriment to him and his future relationship with the child were the application granted?*

(e) *To what extent would that be offset by extension of the child's relationship with the maternal family and homeland?*

(f) *What would be the impact on the Mother, either as a single parent or as a new wife, of a refusal of her realistic proposal?*

Alongside these questions there must be overriding consideration of the child's welfare as the court's paramount consideration, directed by the welfare checklist.

Paragraph 85 of the judgement set out key points that require consideration;

(a) *The welfare of the child is always paramount;*

(b) *There is not presumption in favour of the applicant parent;*

(c) *The reasonable proposals of the parent with a residence order wishing to live abroad carry great weight;*

(d) *The proposals of the parents have to be scrutinised with care and the court needs to be satisfied that there is a genuine motivation for the move and not the intention to bring contact between the child and other parent to an end;*

(e) *The effect upon the applicant parent and the new family of the child if the application is refused is very important;*

(f) *The effect upon the child of the denial of contact with the other parent and in some cases his family is very significant;*

(g) *The opportunity for continuing contact between the child and the left behind parent may be very significant.*

It was highlighted that these comments were on the premise that the question of residence was not in dispute. If the residence of a child is in dispute and this is finely balanced, then the future plans for the parents are clearly relevant and an important factor that must be taken in to consideration. In this matter, the Judge noted the issue of residence was clear and in these circumstances the issue of removal from the jurisdiction would be unlikely to impact upon the decision of residence.

The Court of Appeal held the Judge in the first instance had given a 'careful and excellent judgement' dealing with all of the relevant considerations and did not agree there had been a presumption in favour of the applicant, and that paramount consideration to the child's welfare had been given. The Judge was entitled to come to the conclusion that the effect on the Mother to have to remain in England would be devastating to her and this would be damaging to the child, and that the Father and child could mitigate any impact by contact taking place 2-3 times per year. The Father's appeal was therefore dismissed.

<u>Re: Y (leave to remove from jurisdiction) [2004] 2 FLR 330</u>

The Mother, who was from the United States applied to return there with the party's child, whom was 5 ½ at the date of the hearing following the end of her marriage and divorce.

The parties had a shared care arrangement, with the child spending almost exactly equal time with both parents.

In giving judgement the court said that as the parents shared equal care the guidance of Payne did not apply and the matter should be decided on the welfare checklist. The Mother's application was refused finding that, although the Mother's plans were "*genuine and reasonable*" and that distress would be caused to the Mother if her application was refused, the disruption to the child and loss of the relationship with the Father was too great and outweighed this.

K v K (children) (removal from jurisdiction) [2011] EWCA Civ 793 [2011] All ER (D) 67 (Jul)

This was an application by a Mother to relocate to Canada with the party's two children, who were aged 2 and 4 at the time of the application. The children were spending time with both parents under a shared residence order, spending five days with the Father and nine with the Mother every fortnight. The Mother relied on a Nanny to care for the children apart from on a Wednesday and weekends. This meant although the Mother had more days with the children the Father actually spent more time caring for them due to being off work on the five days he cared for them.

CAFCASS undertook a report and recommended the Mother's application to relocate should be refused. The Judge at the first instance disagreed with the recommendations, granting permission to the Mother. The Father subsequently appealed on three grounds;

1. The Judge had failed to give a proper explanation and reasons for not following the CAFCASS report;

2. The Judge should have followed the guidance from the case of Re: Y (leave to remove from jurisdiction) [2004] 2 FLR 330 as opposed to the guidance from Payne as the parties shared equal care of the children, and;

3. The Judge had failed to consider the case properly as the judgement only made reference to the Mother's application, and therefore had failed to consider the case of the Father.

Thorpe LJ thought all three grounds for appeal had been made out. Black LJ disagreed on the second ground and Moore-Bick LJ was more general in his decision. The appeal was however allowed.

This case should be cited by practitioners where parents share equal care of the children, distinguishing the case from the Payne guidance.

Re: F (a child) (permission to relocate) [2012] EWCA Civ 1364 [2013] 1 FLR 645

Both parents were Spanish and moved to the UK due to the Father's work. After two years in the UK the Father's contract for employment was extended but the parties were having difficulties and their relationship was coming to an end. The parties travelled to Spain for a holiday and after a few days of being back in the UK the Mother returned to Spain. The child remained with the Father, which the Mother believed would be for a short period. The Father issued an application in the courts of England and Wales for a residence order. The Mother made a similar application before the Spanish courts, before issuing an application in the English and Welsh High Court under the Hague Convention.

The High Court Judge concluded the child was habitually residence in the UK at the relevant date and so the courts of England and Wales held jurisdiction. The Mother's application for a return to Spain was therefore refused.

A shared residence order was granted, as was the Mother's application to relocate to Spain with the child. The Father was ordered regular contact in the UK.

The Judge in the first instance described the matter as 'finely balanced, and noted the child would have advantages both living in the UK and in Spain.

In giving judgement and granting the Mother's application to relocate, Judge Marston referenced the Payne guidance, stating the Mother's application was *"genuinely motivated"* and *"realistic"*, the Father's opposition was, *"motivated by genuine concern for the future of his child's welfare,"* and that he had considered, 'the detriment to the Father and his future relationship with the child.'

The Judge said in applying the Payne guidance he was left with a finely balanced case, and then went on to apply the welfare checklist.

The Father appealed on the grounds the Judge erred in applying the guidance in Payne v Payne, which he said did not apply as the Father was the primary carer at the time of the application, and so the parent seeking permission to relocate was not the primary carer. It was submitted that the guidance from K v K also did not apply, as K v K related to a shared residence matter. It was submitted the Judge had failed to give consideration to the status quo, in that the Father was the primary carer and also that the child was residing and settled in the UK.

In giving judgement Munby LJ, as he was then, stated that the starting point should be K v K, in that *"the only principle to be applied when determining an application to remove a child permanently from the jurisdiction was that the welfare of the child was paramount and overbore all other considerations however powerful and reasonable they might be"*.

The Father's appeal was refused with Munby LJ finding there had been no error in law, and the Judge in the first instance was entitled to look at the Payne guidance, but his decision had been based on the best interests of the child.

Munby LJ emphasised Black LJ's comments in K v K, that the court should not get bogged down in whether a case was a Payne v Payne case or a Re: Y case. Munby LJ concluded his judgement with these comments which provide helpful and clear guidance;

> *"The focus from beginning to end must be on the child's best interests. The child's welfare is paramount. Every case must be determined having regard to the "welfare checklist", though of course also having regard, where relevant and helpful, to such guidance as may have been given by this court."*

Re: F (a child) (international relocation cases) [2015] EWCA Civ 882 [2015] All ER (D) 90 (Aug)

The Mother sought permission to relocate permanently to Germany with the party's 12-year old child. The Father appealed the decision of the first instance court in granting permission to the Mother to relocate.

The Father appealed and this was subsequently granted on the grounds the Judge had made an error in law by applying only some of the Payne guidance.

The Court of Appeal provided clarification on the current law on external relocation applications. This is summarised in paragraphs 86, 96 and 140 to 145 of the Judgement from K v K, which affirmed the judgement of Re: F.

The current law and guidance is;

- The only principle that must be followed is that the child's welfare is the court's paramount consideration, everything else, including the Payne guidance, is just that 'guidance' and consideration of this should be based on how it will impact on the child;

- The Payne guidance should not be ignored, but must be considered as guidance, not as a rigid principle;

- The Payne guidance is to be read alongside the other factors, not given priority over them;

- Partial citation or selecting only some of the guidance points from Payne is likely to be an error in law;

- There is no presumption in favour of either parent, and the reasonable proposals of the parent with a residence order wishing to live abroad carry 'great weight,' whereas the effect on the child of denying contact with the other parent is 'very important';

- The decision in Re: Y is not a different line of authority as set out in Payne v Payne, and the decision of Re: Y still falls within the Payne framework. The identification of whether parents have shared care, or whether one parent is the primary carer simply highlights how the weight attached to the relevant factors alters depending upon the facts of the case;

- Cases should not get bogged down as to whether they were Payne v Payne cases or Re: Y cases;

- When determining relocation cases *"all of the facts need to be considered"*;

- The court must take a *"holistic approach"* weighing up the pros and cons of the positions of both parties, not just the parent seeking to relocate.

Although the checklist from Payne should be considered it is by no means determinative and any argument either for or against a relocation application should be based around the welfare of the child, looking at the welfare checklist.

Current case law would suggest the guidance in Payne will apply where the parent seeking to relocate is the child's primary carer, however this is only guidance, not an exhaustive checklist. In cases where the parent seeking to relocate is not the child's primary carer, or where parents equally share care there are differing views on whether the Payne guidance should apply. Re: F (a child) (permission to relocate) would suggest it does still apply with Munby J stating that the Payne guidance may be utilised in relocation cases where an application is not by the primary carer if the judge thinks it is appropriate and helpful to do so.

e. Returning a Child Unilaterally Removed Externally

It is not possible to do justice and cover external child abduction fully in one chapter and this would require a book of its own. However, the first starting point should be looking at whether the country to where the child has been removed is a Hague Convention country. If the child has been removed to a Hague Convention country, then an application can be made under the Convention for their return. Member states will then co-operate to implement any orders made.

If the removal is to a country that is not a Hague Convention country then the first question would be determining where jurisdiction is held. If the children have been removed from England and Wales to a non-Hague Convention country then an application should be made to seek the court's inherent jurisdiction, meaning they effectively retain control over the matter. Applications can then be made to the High Court for the return of the children and steps made to enforce the order in the jurisdiction where the child has been taken / retained. The exact steps will depend upon the relevant law and authorities in that county.

There is a wealth of guidance issued but a good starting point is the Foreign and Commonwealth Office's Guardian: 'Foreign and Commonwealth Office: International parental child abduction.' There was also guidance issued by Sir James Munby in April 2016, 'President of the Family Division; Liaison between Courts in England and Wales and British Embassies and High Commissions Abroad.'

f. Contact with the Remaining Parent

Where the court grant permission for a permanent external relocation, they are agreeing that the child will be brought up in another culture and under another country's legal systems and legislation. The English and Welsh courts are effectively surrendering jurisdiction. On that basis it is often inappropriate to make orders for contact as this is contrary to the surrendering of jurisdiction unless this is with the purpose of making an order with the purpose of having this mirrored in the new jurisdiction.

In Re: N (leave to remove from jurisdiction) (No. 2) [2014] EWHC B16 the Mother was applying to relocate and return to Tanzania where the maternal family continued to reside. The Father was having weekly contact with the child, supervised by the paternal grandparents due to concerns about his illicit drug use.

The Father opposed the Mother's application to relocate and sought further contact.

The Mother's application to relocate was granted, with the judge referring to the guidance from Payne and that the child's welfare was the court's paramount consideration. It was found the Mother's application was realistic and not motivated by wanting to cut the Father or his family out of the child's life, and her proposals were sensible and realistic.

A family assistance order was made for a period of three months to assist with parental communication and contact arrangements between them.

In Re: R (leave to remove: contact) [2011] 1 FLR 1336 although the judge approved the Mother's contact proposals with her plan to relocate to Australia no contact order was made. The Father issued an appeal on three grounds;

1. The court should have directed a CAFCASS report;
2. The judge could have made a defined contact order;
3. The judge should have identified evidence in support of his conclusion that the Mother would suffer harm if not permitted to relocate.

In addressing point 2 the judge said;

> *"Although a contact order is, as I have noticed, now occasionally made by way of attachment to a grant of leave, it is contrary to principle. A contact order would be an order taking effect until further order of the English court. But, on a grant of leave, the English court is, if only for*

practical reasons, surrendering its control over the child to the foreign court."

It was highlighted that, should the Mother not provide the child for contact as set out in her proposal the Father would be making an application to the Australian courts once relocation had taken place. Had the judge not considered the Mother's contact proposals, the Father would have had reasonable grounds for appeal, but as the judge did take these in to consideration in their decision there was no error.

g. Key Legislation

As has been confirmed in the above Court of Appeal cases of K v K, Re: F (a child) (permission to relocate) and Re: F (a child) (international relocation cases) the key, and in fact only factor the court must consider is Section 1(1) Children Act 1989, the child's welfare is the court's paramount consideration.

Section 1(3) Children Act 1989 provides the welfare checklist which the court will consider when determining what is in the child's best interests. Chapter 4 on internal relocation provides this checklist.

Section 1(4) Children Act 1989 requires the court to have consideration of the welfare checklist when making, varying or discharging any order under Section 8 of the children act, which includes a Child Arrangements Order, Prohibited Steps order and / or Specific Issue Order. This would be the orders that either prevent or grant permission for a child relocation.

Section 13(1) Children Act 1989 prohibits the removal of a child from the jurisdiction without the written consent of every person who holds Parental Responsibility. This is subject to Section 13(2) which permits the removal of a child for a period of up to one month by any person with whom a child lives under a Child Arrangements Order, or for a period of up to three months by any person named as a Special Guardian under a court order.

h. Case Law

The main cases providing the key guidance on external relocation cases have already been stated above, but the following may also be useful for reference.

Poel v Poel [1970] 1 WLR 1469

Following the party's divorce the Mother had remarried and was expecting her second child. She was seeking permission to relocate with her new husband to New Zealand, taking the party's two-year old son with her. After the application was initially refused the Mother successfully appealed.

The appeal was granted on the grounds that, when determining any application to relocate or remove a child from the jurisdiction, the court's primary consideration was the welfare of the child and whether it was in the child's best interests to grant the application. This would include giving consideration to the welfare of the parent who was the primary carer, and noting that if they were unhappy this could potentially adversely impact upon the child.

This decision and guidance has been cited and confirmed in a number of cases since.

Tyler v Tyler [1989] 2 FLR 158

Although pre-dating the case of Payne by a number of years, this confirms that where a parent's application to relocate is motivated by a desire to exclude the other parent from the child's life, it must be refused.

The court refused the Mother's application to relocate to Australia. The judge in the first instance stating in his judgement;

> *'I am driven to the conclusion that her behaviour with regard to access, and the bitterness and negative feelings that she admittedly had towards her ex-husband, were mainly motivated by her desire to improve her chances of getting to Australia and by the thought that, if*

> *she made access more difficult, she would weaken the bonds between the Father and sons.'*

The judge had concluded the Mother's motive for seeking to relocate was due to the bitterness towards the Father, despite the fact she had family living in Australia.

In considering the Mother's appeal Kerr LJ said the judge had been entitled to reach these conclusions and considered all of the relevant circumstances. The appeal was refused.

Re: B (children) (removal from jurisdiction);
Re: S (a child) (removal from jurisdiction) [2003] 2 FLR 1043

Both cases were heard before the Court of Appeal to consider applications by the Mothers to relocate to their countries of origin and to continue new relationships, one wishing to move to South Africa to continue a relationship with an affluent businessman and the other wanting to move to Australia to marry.

Both appeals were allowed on the grounds the court must give due recognition of the realities and also dangers of obstructing the reasonable proposals of the primary carer, as well as consideration needing to be given to the impact of the child if the court's decision jeopardised the prospects of survival of the family by frustrating the family's natural emigration.

H v F (refusal of leave to remove a child from the jurisdiction) [2005] EWHC 2705 (Fam)

This case applied and confirmed the guidance from Payne that if the relocating parent's plans are not realistic and well thought out then the application must fail.

The Mother applied to permanently relocate to Jamaica, her country of birth to start a Bed and Breakfast. This was opposed by the Father who suggested it was motivated by malice and to obstruct his relationship with the child, as he had recently remarried and also that the plan to start a

Bed and Breakfast in Jamaica was not well thought out and in the child's best interests. The court held that although there was considerable hostility by the Mother towards the Father, it could not be said her proposals were malicious and an attempt to exclude the Father from the child's life. The court did however still refuse the application on the grounds that the Mother's proposals were "*utterly ill-conceived and, thus, unreasonable*" and this alone was enough to defeat the Mother's application.

Re: N (a child) [2006] All ER (D) 105 (Mar)

A Mother's appeal to remove the child from the jurisdiction unaccompanied for two weeks to stay with the maternal Grandmother and cousin was approved, with the Court of Appeal noting a number of positive factors to the Mother's application;

- Slovakia was a signatory to the Hague Convention;
- This would maintain the child's Slovakian heritage;
- The court welfare officer approved the visit;
- The first instance judgement should have looked at matters through the eyes of the child.

Re: F & H (children) [2007] EWCA Civ 880

The Mother's application to relocate to the USA with the children was approved, and subsequently appealed by the Father on the grounds the Mother had not provided clear plans for the children, such as schooling and financial income. The Father's appeal was refused and the court held that where a primary carer is returning to a completely familiar environment, the bar was set much lower, especially where the Mother was returning to a completely familiar home life.

Re: W [2008] (children) (leave to remove) [2008] 2 FLR 1170

The court granted an application by a Mother to return to Sweden with the party's three children due to her husband's income being insufficient to sustain the family's lifestyle.

This also highlighted that the decision in relocation cases is always fact-dependent.

Re: W [2009] All ER (D) 120 (May)

The Mother applied to permanently relocate to New Zealand with the party's two children as her new partner, had obtained employment there. The Mother's application was refused describing her partners attempts to obtain work in the UK as "*half-hearted*" and finding that the Mother would not actively encourage the Father's relationship and contact with the children if she were permitted to relocate.

The Court of Appeal refused the Mother's appeal finding that the judge had approached the evidence in a methodical and sensible manner, and whilst considering the impact on the Mother if her application were refused, he did not believe she would be "*emotionally damaged*" and that she had not considered the loss of the wider family upon the children and that her contact proposals with the Father were unrealistic.

Re: TC and JC (children: relocation) [2013] EWHC 292 (Fam) All ER (D) 316 (Feb)

In paragraph 11 of his judgement, Mostyn J set out what he considered to be the govering principles for relocation applications;

> *i) The only authentic principle to be applied when determining an application to relocate a child permanently overseas is that the welfare of the child is paramount and overbears all other considerations, however powerful and reasonable they might be;*
>
> *ii) The guidance given by the Court of Appeal as to the factors to be weighed in search of the welfare paramountcy, and which directs the*

exercise of the welfare discretion, is valuable. Such guidance helps the judge to identify which factors are likely to be the most important and the weight which should generally be attached to them, and, incidentally, promotes consistency in decision-making;

iii) The guidance is not confined to classic primary carer applications and may be utilised in other kinds of relocation cases if the judge thinks it helpful and appropriate to do so;

iv) The guidance suggests that the following questions be asked and answered (assuming that the applicant is the Mother);

> *a) Is the Mother's application genuine in the sense that it is not motivated by some selfish desire to exclude the Father from the child's life?*
>
> *b) Is the Mother's application realistically founded on practical proposals both well researched and investigated?*
>
> *c) What would be the impact on the Mother, either as the single parent or as a new wife, of a refusal of her realistic proposal?*
>
> *d) Is the Father's opposition motivated by genuine concern for the future of the child's welfare or is it driven by some ulterior motive?*
>
> *e) What would be the extent of the detriment to him and his future relationship with the child were the application granted?*
>
> *f) To what extent would that detriment be offset by extension of the child's relationships with the maternal family and homeland?*

v) Since the circumstances in which such decisions have to be made vary infinitely and the judge in each case has to be free to decide whatever is in the best interests of the child, such guidance should not be applied rigidly as if it contains principles from which no departure is permitted;

> *vi) There is no legal principle, let alone some legal or evidential presumption, in favour of an application to relocate by a primary carer. The old statements which seem to favour applications to relocate made by primary carers are no more than a reflection of the reality of the human condition and the parent-child relationship;*
>
> *vii) The hearing must not get mired in taxonomical arguments or preliminary skirmishes as to what label should be applied to the case by virtue of either the time spent with each of the parents or other aspects of the care arrangements.*

It was noted that there should be no difference in applications where a parent is seeking to relocate for a better life or where they are seeking to return to a country of origin, however if it is a location where a child is familiar, then this will be a relevant consideration and the harm to a child lessened. There will be a lower threshold where a child is moving to somewhere familiar in comparison to moving somewhere that they have no prior knowledge or experience of.

H (Mother) v C (Father) and another [2015] EWCA Civ 1298 [2016] All ER (D) 11 (Jan)

This related to an application by the Mother to permanently relocate with the party's child to New York.

The children were aged 15 and 17 the time of the application. In giving judgement, Jackson J considered the no order principle, and whether orders should be made for children of this age. The Judge commented that the court should be cautious in making arrangements for children of that age. It was directed that the shared residence order made in 2006, which required the parents to review arrangements should one of them wish to reside in another jurisdiction, would expire when the youngest child attained 16.

X, Y and Z (children) (retrospective leave to remove from the jurisdiction) [2016] EWHC 2439 (Fam)

This was an application by a Mother for retrospective permission three years after the children had been taken from the UK to Spain. The Father had no contact with the children after their removal to Spain, and obtained Hague Convention orders requiring the Mother to return the children to the UK. The Mother had applied for permission to relocate with the children to Spain.

The Judge directed the English and Welsh courts should hear the application, noting that there had been lengthy delays due to the Spanish processes. Despite the fact it was accepted the children had been resident in Spain for the last three years, as the court felt the Father had acted promptly in seeking their return and orders to this effect had been made under the Hague Convention the English and Welsh courts held jurisdiction.

Re: M (children) (permission to relocate) [2016] EWCA Civ 1059 [2016] All ER (D) 58 (Nov)

In granting the Mother's application to relocate to Russia and dismissing the Father's appeal, the court stated there was only one principle in relocation cases. The welfare of the child is the court's paramount consideration. Everything else is just *"guidance"* and can be assistance or not to the judge depending on the circumstances of the cases.

F v L [2017] EWHC 1377 (Fam) [2017] All ER (D) 63 (Jun)

In addition to the Mother's application to permanently relocate to Italy, both parents issued cross applications to decide with whom the child should live with and where their primary residence should be.

The Mother's appeal against the refusal to grant permission to relocate was granted. It was emphasised that before determining the issue of relocation, the Judge should have determined the living arrangements for the child, describing that the Judge effectively, *"had started off where should ought to have concluded."*

L v F [2017] EWCA Civ 2121]2018] All ER (D) 83 (Jan)

When the above proceedings concluded before the Court of Appeal, they emphasised and confirmed that the court should adopt a holistic and global approach, considering each of the options before them (and in this case the court had 5 different options to consider), looking at the pros and cons of each.

Contrary to the High Court's comments the Court of Appeal made it clear that it was not necessary or appropriate to determine the child's living arrangements before determining the issue of relocation, and in fact the issues were inherently interconnected and should be considered together.

The requirement to undertake a holistic approach was also further emphasised in the case of JAL v LSW [2017] EWHC 3699 (Fam) [2017] All ER (D) 141 (Dec).

S v S [2017] EWHC 2345 (Fam) [2017] All ER (D) 71 (Oct)

The Father was seeking permission to take the party's two boys, aged 13 and 15 to live with him and his new partner, along with their child to Switzerland. The application was opposed by the children's Mother, who was their primary carer and lived in England. The court appointed a guardian to represent the children given their ages and ability to provide instructions.

The court held that although a change in primary carer, by placing the children with their Father would be a change in circumstance, the move to Switzerland would be less of a change as the children had moved around the world, having previously lived in three different countries already.

The children's educational needs would be met in Switzerland, with their schooling unlikely to be worse than what they were currently receiving. The Father was also able to meet the children's emotional and physical needs.

The court found the children were unlikely to lose the relationship with their Mother as the Father had proposed financial provisions and a plan to continue contact and their relationship, including offering to fund a property for the Mother in Switzerland.

Re: C (a child) [2019] EWHC 131 (Fam) [2019] All ER (D) 154 (Jan)

The Mother's application to permanently relocate with the child from the UK to Africa was refused. She issued an appeal on eight grounds. The Mother's appeal was allowed on the grounds the judge had not carried out a *"holistic evaluaton"*. This emphasised that a Judge should consider all possible options available, weighing up the pros and cons of each.

CAFCASS reports

The following cases give guidance on CAFCASS reports.

Re: T (a child) (CA, 19 November 2015, unreported)

This confirmed the court can make a decision without a CAFCASS report and this is not always necessary, and in some cases this may not be helpful, and may in fact be a misuse of court resources.

Re: R (leave to remove: contact) [2011] 1 FLR 1336

More details on this case are provided earlier in this chapter, but ground 3 of the Father's appeal was on the basis the judge should have ordered a CAFCASS report.

The Court of Appeal confirmed the ordering of a CAFCASS report was down to the judge's discretion and was not always necessary in determining matters.

Re: E (relocation: removal from jurisdiction) [2013] 2 FLR 290

A CAFCASS report was undertaken that made recommendations the Mother's application to relocate to the USA to continue a relationship with someone she met on the internet, taking the party's children aged 5 and 11 with her, be refused. The judge granted the Mother's application on the basis she obtain a mirrored order in America. The Father appealed on the grounds the Judge went against the CAFCASS recommendations.

His appeal was unsuccessful and it was noted that the Judge is entitled to depart from the recommendations and had given reasons for doing so, finding that the CAFCASS officer had failed to take into account the quality of the Mother's proposals for contact, and that the report lacked the necessary bredth and was not a balanced report.

Re: L (relocation: second appeal) [2018] 2 FLR 608

The CAFCASS officer's report suggested there were no reasons for the Mother's application to relocate to Italy not to be granted. It was suggested the loss of the relationship between the child and his Father could be addressed through indirect contact. The Judge did not agree with this, stating that the CAFCASS officer was unable to give any positives to the move apart from this addressing the Mother's unhappiness, and the Judge felt the child's welfare did require him to maintain a relationship with his Father.

Again the court departed from the recommendations in the CAFCASS report, but gave reasons for doing so.

In giving judgement Peter Jackson J quoted Hale LJ in the case of *Re: J (Residence: Expert Evidence)* [2001] 2 FCR 44;

> *"It is of course well-established that, if there are professional witnesses who have been asked to advise the court by way of a section 7 report, the court should at least do those witnesses the courtesy of explaining clearly the reasons for departing from their recommendations (although it has always been acknowledged that the court has the power to do that)."*

The above cases confirm the court can depart from the recommendations of a CAFCASS report as long as they give reasons for doing so and that any decision is ultimately in the best interests of the child.

Meeting with the children

The following cases looked at obtaining the children's wishes and feelings, including the Judge meeting the children and the children giving evidence.

Re: N-A (children) [2017] All ER (D) 143 (Apr) [2017] EWCA Civ 230

This was an application by the Father to relocate to Iran with the party's sons who were aged 16 and 13 at the date of the appeal. His application was refused and the Father subsequently issued an appeal and this too was unsuccessful.

The guidance from this case relates to obtaining the children's wishes and feelings, from the Judge meeting with the children.

In her meeting with the children, they expressed a wish to move to Iran with their Father, which they had been consistent about throughout the proceedings. The Judge however had formed the view that the children had been influenced by their Father and although they knew what Iran was like from the time they had previously spent there, they did not really understand what a permanent move and living there would be like.

The Father's appeal was on the grounds that the Judge had given insufficient weight to the children's wishes and feelings and that she had gathered evidence which she had relied upon in her decision, which was contrary to the Family Justice Counsel 'Guidelines for Judges Meeting Children who are Subject to Family Proceedings (2010).' It was also stated the Judge had not informed the parties of the impressions she had formed of the children so this could be explored in evidence and submissions.

The relevant part of the guidance upon which the Father's appeal was based is paragraph 5 which states;

> *"It cannot be stressed too often that the child's meeting with the judge is not for the purpose of gathering evidence. That is the responsibility*

> *of the Cafcass officer. The purpose is to enable the child to gain some understanding of what is going on, and to be reassured that the judge has understood him/her."*

Where consideration is being given to a meeting between the Judge and a child practitioners should refer to these guidelines, which although only consisting of two pages provides very clear guidance on best practice.

A Father v A Mother [2017] EWFC 48 [2017] All ER (D) 200 (Jul)

The application to relocate was in this matter made by the child, whom was aged 14 at the time. His application was subsequently taken on by his Father.

The child was living with his Mother and step-Father in the UK and applied to live with his Father who may be moving to *"an identified Scandinavian country"*. The child was deemed as competent and able to instruct his own solicitor.

It was agreed the child would give evidence, however; not that he would be cross examined by his parents. The court therefore directed each parent would prepare five questions to be put to the child by the Judge, with his solicitor also asking him five questions as opening.

Although the child was clear in his wishes and feelings, the application was refused on the grounds the Father had lost sight of what was best for the child. He had not given clear plans, and it was not even known if he would be moving. The Judge was therefore not confident any move would work. The court also made a Section 91(14) order, prohibiting future court applications and effectively confirming the child's circumstances would remain unchanged until he was at an age whereby he could make his own decisions outside of the court's jurisdiction and powers.

The judgement was given in the form of a letter addressed to the child directly.

Although highly unusual for a child to be the one issuing the application, this case highlights how the court can be flexible to allow a child to give evidence and also amend proceedings to be child focused and orientated.

CL v AL [2017] EWHC 2154 (Fam) [2017] All ER (D) 117 (Oct)

The court had to consider the conflicting wishes and feelings of two children. The eldest child, aged 13 was living in England with the Father. The youngest, aged 10 was living in Australia with the Mother. Both parents agreed the children should live together with one parent, but both wanting the children to live with them.

The eldest was adamant he did not wish to live in Australia, but did want to live with his younger brother. The youngest had expressed that he did not want to live in England, wanting to remain in Australia.

It was clear one child would be disappointed and the court needed to weigh up the strength of the children's wishes and feelings, and impact upon them if the court were to go against their clearly expressed wishes. In weighing up the balance of harm the court found that the younger brother's views were not as strong as those of his elder brother and therefore the harm to him would be less. The court therefore found in favour of the elder sibling's wishes, ordering both children reside with the Father in England.

CHAPTER SIX

PROCEDURE

Urgent and Without Notice Applications

It is hard to see a situation where an urgent application for permission to relocate would be required, and even more difficult to envisage one that would be granted.

The type of application required would depend on whether there is an existing Child Arrangements Order in force.

If there is a risk that notice to the other parent will result in a move prior to the matter going before the court, an urgent without notice application can be issued. Part 12 of the Family Procedure Rules 2010 covers Children Act Proceedings and Rule 12.16 applications without notice. Rule 12.16(5) FPR 2010 requires any application and order to be served upon the Respondent within 48 hours of any order being made. Rules 12.2 and 12.3 outline the circumstances where without notice orders should be made.

Rules 12.2 and 12.3 Family Procedure Rules 2010

Rule 12.2

'Without Notice': Applications to court made 'Without Notice' to the respondent(s) shall be allocated in accordance with the Family Court (Composition and Distribution of Business) Rules 2014, and determined by reference to the provisions of Practice Direction 18A, paragraph 5.1, with further regard to the principles set out in Practice Direction 20A, paragraph 4.3-4.5 FPR (noting particularly paragraph 4.3(c)).

Rule 12.3

Without Notice Orders should be made only exceptionally, and where –

> *(1) If the applicant were to give notice to the respondent(s) this would enable the respondent(s) to take steps to defeat the purpose of the injunction; cases where the application is brought without notice in order to conceal the step from the respondent(s) are very rare indeed; or*
>
> *(2) The case is one of exceptional urgency; that is to say, that there has been literally no time to give notice (either by telephone, text or e-mail or otherwise) before the injunction is required to prevent the threatened wrongful act; or*
>
> *(3) If the applicant gives notice to the respondent(s), this would be likely to expose the applicant or relevant child to unnecessary risk of physical or emotional harm.*

If an application is made on notice this is governed by Rules 12.3 – 12.15 of the FPR 2010.

If a parent has already moved with the child the practical considerations of a return will need to be considered if that parent no longer has accommodation available. The court can order the return of the child, including a change of residence to enable the child to remain in the same location.

Prevention of a move is however often easier than seeking a return.

<u>Issue up to First Hearing Dispute Resolution Appointment (FHDRA)</u>

An application for permission to externally relocate should be considered by a High Court judge as this will often require consideration and knowledge of the legal system and processes of a foreign jurisdiction, as well as obtaining a mirrored order.

Once issued the same procedure would be followed for both applications where a Child Arrangements Order is and is not in place.

Although the procedure will be the same irrespective of whether or not a Child Arrangements Order is in force, if there is an order the application may be for a variation of the existing order rather than a new Specific Issue Order. The same procedure will also apply whether the party is seeking permission to relocate or seeking to prevent a relocation. The only addition would be if this included an urgent application for the return of a child who has already been removed.

Part 12 of the Family Procedure Rules 2010 sets out the procedure for private Children Act proceedings.

The application either for permission to relocate under a Specific Issue Order, variation of a Child Arrangements Order, or to prevent a relocation under a Prohibited Steps Order (or a Specific Issue Order for return if the child(ren) has already been removed) would be made on a C100 and potentially a C1A if allegations of harm or abduction are being alleged.

A copy of the application will need to be served upon every person whom the applicant knows, or believes holds Parental Responsibility.

If the relocation is internal this is likely to be allocated to District Judge level and can be heard in the court local to where the child resides.

Rule 12.5 FPR 2010 sets out the procedure the court will follow once an application has been issued.

Rule 12.5 Family Procedure Rules 2010

> *(1) When proceedings other than public law proceedings have been issued the court will consider –*
>
> *(a) setting a date for –*
>
> *(i) a directions appointment;*

(ii) in private law proceedings, a First Hearing Dispute Resolution Appointment; or

(iii) omitted;

(iv) the hearing of the application;

and if the court sets a date it will do so in accordance with rule 12.13 and Practice Direction 12B;

(b) giving any of the directions listed in rule 12.12 or, where Chapter 6, section 1 applies, rule 12.48; and

(c) doing anything else which is set out in Practice Direction 12B or any other practice direction.

(2) When Part 4 proceedings and in so far as practicable other public law proceedings have been issued the court will –

(a) set a date for the Case Management Hearing in accordance with Practice Direction 12A;

(b) set a date for the hearing of an application for an interim order if necessary;

(c) give any directions listed in rule 12.12; and

(d) do anything else which is set out in Practice Direction 12A.

Practice Direction 12B FPR 2010 sets out the timetable to be followed by the court specifically rules 9.1 – 9.4 dealing with allocation and gatekeeping. Under rule 9.2 a court application should be considered by a nominated legal advisor and / or nominated District Judge within one working day of receipt. Rule 9.4 allows the gatekeeper to issue directions upon allocation. This would usually include CAFCASS being required to undertake safeguarding checks (Rules 13.1 – 13.8). Under Rule 13.7 CAFCASS safeguarding checks should be completed within 17 working days of CAFCASS receiving the application and no less than 3 weeks before the first hearing. The gatekeeper can give directions for an accelerated hearing where they believe the matter is urgent, but it would be sensible to flag this in the application in the first instance.

Rule 22 of FPR 2010 sets out the court timetable;

- Working day 1 – Court paperwork received and checked by the court office to ensure it is completed correctly and in full;

- Working Day 3 – The case is considered by the Gatekeeping team and allocated and the court send a copy of the application to CAFCASS to undertake their safeguarding checks;

- 17 working days from receipt of the application – CAFCASS complete and file their safeguarding checks;

- No later than 6 weeks after receipt of the paperwork – case listed for FHDRA

Rule 11.1 outlines the key welfare principles, emphasising what is contained in Section 1 Children Act 1989, with Rule 11.2 outlining the key parts of the Family Procedure Rules that may apply.

Rule 11.1 Family Procedure Rules 2010

> *Section 1 of the Children Act 1989 applies to all applications for orders concerning the upbringing of children. This means that –*
>
> *(1) the child's welfare is the court's paramount consideration;*
>
> *(2) delay is likely to be prejudicial to the welfare of the child; and*
>
> *(3) a court order shall not be made unless the court considers that making an order would be better for the child than making no order at all.*

Rule 11.2 Family Procedure Rules 2010

Parties, and the court, must also have regard to the FPR in particular the following –

(1) FPR Rule 1. The 'overriding objective' will apply, so that the court will deal with a case justly, having regard to the welfare issues involved and specifically will –

(a) Ensure that the case is dealt with expeditiously and fairly;

(b) Deal with the case in ways which are proportionate to the nature, importance and complexity of the issues;

(c) Ensure that the parties are on an equal footing;

(d) Save expense;

(e) Allot to each case an appropriate share of the court's resources, while taking account of the need to allot resources to other cases.

(2) Rule 3, and Practice Direction 3A;

(3) FPR Part 4 'General Case Management Powers';

(4) FPR Part 15 (Representation of Protected Parties) and Practice Direction 15B (Adults Who May Be Protected Parties and Children Who May Become Protected Parties in Family Proceedings);

(5) FPR Part 16 (Representation of Children) (and see also paragraph 18 below);

(6) FPR Part 18 (procedure for Other Applications in proceedings);

(7) FPR Part 22 (Evidence);

(8) Omitted;

(9) FPR Part 25 (Experts) and the Experts Practice Directions;

(10) FPR 27.6 and Practice Direction 27A (Court Bundles).

Following issue of the application notice would need to be given to any person who has care and control of the child(ren) and / or who holds Parental Responsibility and they should be listed as a Respondent in any court application.

First Hearing Dispute Resolution Appointment (FHDRA)

This is governed under Rule 14 of the FPR 2010.

An FHDRA should take place within at least 6 weeks following the issuing of the application, with the Respondent(s) receiving at least 14 days' notice of the hearing, with the court having permission to shorten this notice period.

Rules 14.8 and 14.11 outline the purpose of the FHDRA, being assisting the parties in identifying the issues and seeing if an agreement can be reached.

Rule 14.8 FPR 2010

The FHDRA provides an opportunity for the parties to be helped to an understanding of the issues which divide them, and to reach agreement. If agreement is reached –

(1) The Court will be able to make an order (which in many cases will be a final order) reflecting that agreement;

(2) The Court will assist the parties (so far as it is able) in putting into effect the agreement/order in a co-operative way.

Rule 14.11 FPR 2010

At the FHDRA the judge, working with the Cafcass Officer, or WFPO, will seek to assist the parties in conciliation and in resolution of all or any of the issues between them. Any remaining issues will be identified, the Cafcass Officer or WFPO will advise the court of any recommended means of resolving such issues, and directions will be

> *given for the future resolution of such issues. At all times the decisions of the Court and the work of the Cafcass Officer or WFPO will take account of any risk or safeguarding issues that have been identified.*

Rule 14.13 provides a number of matters the court should consider including;

- Safeguarding;
- Mediation and Alternative Dispute Resolution;
- Consent Orders;
- Reports;
- Wishes and Feelings of the Child;
- Case Management / directions;
- Allocation;
- The order required to progress matters.

Practitioners should refer to rule 14.13 which provides a detailed breakdown on each of the above headings.

Any parent seeking permission to relocate should direct the court to Rule 15.2 which requires the Judge to consider 'important landmarks' in the life of a child. This includes;

(a) Birthdays;

(b) The start of nursery / school;

(c) The start / end of the school term / year;

(d) Any proposed change of a school.

Whilst not always practical the court should give consideration, particularly in relocation cases to timetabling so any change of school can take place at a time that will cause as little disruption as possible to the child(ren).

In relocation cases the court is likely to require CAFCASS to undertake a Section 7 report outlining their recommendations. This will include consideration of the Section 1(3) Children Act 1989 'Welfare Checklist', including the wishes and feelings of the child(ren) (where possible), the contact that would continue to take place with the other parent if permission to relocate was granted, the life that the child would have if permission was granted, or refused, and providing their recommendations on the application.

Parties are likely to be directed to file statements of evidence prior to the Section 7 report being filed to enable the author to consider these. The court should specify on the face of any order what needs to be covered in these statements. These will need to set out the orders they are asking the court to make, as well as a detailed plan and supporting evidence by the party seeking permission to relocate. The points a party should consider are addressed in chapter 3. Parties can be directed to file simultaneous statements or the relocating party filing their statement first and the other party then filing a statement in response. This very much comes down to the preference of the individual Judge.

The court will need to consider at the FHDRA, as well as throughout proceedings if a fact-finding hearing is necessary. If so, this is likely to be listed prior to the Dispute Resolution Appointment for the court to establish a factual matrix upon which CAFCASS can base their Section 7 report.

Dispute Resolution Appointment (DRA)

The court is likely to list the matter for a DRA following CAFCASS completing their Section 7 report. The timescales for filing this will depend on the area but is usually around 12 weeks. In undertaking this report the CAFCASS officer will speak to both parents and extended family where applicable, as well as the children depending upon the age. This may also involve making enquiries of the children's present and potentially future schools, the Local Authority and such other enquiries as they deem appropriate.

Rule 19.3 FPR 2010 outlines the steps the court are required to take at the DRA, which is effectively to see if the parties can reach an agreement in light of the Section 7 recommendations. If this is still not possible then the matter is likely to be listed through to a final hearing for the court to determine.

The author of the Section 7 report is only required to attend the DRA if ordered by the court (Rule 19.2 FPR 2010), but will almost certainly be required to attend the final hearing as one parent will be challenging their recommendations if parties have been unable to reach an agreement.

Final Hearing

Rule 27 FPR 2010 provides general guidance on hearings and Practice Direction 27A FPR 2010 guidance on court bundles. Rules 4.1, 4.2 and 4.3 PD27A FPR 2010 outline the format of the bundles and what documents should be included.

It is likely parties, as well as family members if they have filed statements, and the author of the Section 7 report, will be required to give evidence. Relevant case law and statutes that the court should consider and apply are addressed in chapters 4 and 5 of this book.

CHAPTER SEVEN

COMPARING INTERNAL AND EXTERNAL RELOCATION AND REMOVAL

Previous precedent had been to treat internal and external relocation cases differently, with the court only refusing applications to internally relocate in exceptional circumstances. This favoured the party seeking to relocate.

However, changes came in 2015 with the judgement in the case of Re: C (A child) (Internal relocation) [2015] EWCA Civ 1305. The Court of Appeal reviewed internal relocation cases and held that there was no basis to distinguish between internal and external relocation cases, and these should be determined using the same criteria.

In giving judgement, Black LJ considered the rationale as to why internal and external relocation cases should be treated differently. Section 13 Children Act 1989, prohibits the removal of any child from the jurisdiction without the written consent of everyone holding parental responsibility. Black LJ noted that this restriction and part of the statute does not refer to being limited to external relocations, and it is the making of a Child Arrangements 'live with' Order that brings this into force.

Consideration was given to Thorpe LJ's comments and judgement in Re: H (Children) (Residence Order) [2001] EWCA Civ 1338 [2001] 2 FLR 1277 with part of his judgement being quoted;

> *"What then is the rationalisation for freer movement of the primary carer within the United Kingdom? It seems to me to be obvious. Within the same sovereignty there will be the same system of laws, with the same rights of the citizen, rights for instance to education, health care and statutory benefits. Equally, it can be said that within Europe, whilst perhaps the burden on the applicant may be greater, it is equally*

> *mitigated by the fact that within the Community there is the same fundamental approach to social issues and a real endeavour to achieve harmonisation, obviously in social policy but also in family justice. If, moving to the third alternative, the application is for relocation outside the European region, the necessary adjustment may be rationalized on the basis that the social and other circumstances involved in relocation may require much greater adjustment for the children; alternatively, that the obstacles to contact may be enhanced. However, attempts to rationalize gradation of the hurdles that the applicant must clear are always liable to be tested by specific example, as this case suggests. What is the rationalisation for a different test to be applied to an application to relocate to Belfast, as opposed to, say, an application to relocate from Gloucester to Dublin? All that the court can do is to remember that in each and every case the decision must rest on the paramount principle of child welfare."*

Black LJ concluded, that although Thorpe LJ considered reasons to differentiate between internal and external relocation, no satisfactory foundation could be found. Black LJ did not agree that the sovereignty of the United Kingdom's laws was a compelling argument, noting that throughout the United Kingdom there are different sets of laws that apply.

Further consideration was given as to whether internal and external relocation is differentiated due to the possibility it may be harder to enforce an order for contact outside of the United Kingdom. However, this too was not agreed, with Black LJ noting that the provisions of Brussels IIA and the 1996 Hague Convention provided provisions for enforcement. Any issue or concerns as to enforceability should form part of the consideration when determining whether an application to relocate should be granted, not distinguishing between internal and external relocations. Since the UK left the EU, the Hague Convention has been acceded into UK law, however, Brussels II has been repealed. The issue of internal and external relocations is yet to be considered following the UK's departure from the EU and inability to rely on Brussels II.

The issue of geographical distance was also addressed, with Black LJ supporting Thorpe LJ's example about relocation to Dublin and Gloucester. This was further highlighted by reference to the case of Re: F (internal relocation) [2010] EWCA Civ 1428 [2011] 1 FLR 1382 where an application was made to relocate to the Orkney Islands and highlighted that an internal relocation could create just as much of a geographical barrier as an external one.

Black LJ too was unable to find a convincing reason as to why internal and external relocation cases were to be treated differently.

After considering a number of cases Black LJ concluded that none of them had been able to find a reason or set a precedent for distinguishing between internal and external relocation cases, stating;

> *"Once welfare has been identified as the governing principle in internal relocation cases, there is no reason to differentiate between those cases and external relocation cases. In my view, the approach set out in* K v K, Re F (Relocation) *[2012] and* Re F *[2015] should apply equally to internal relocation cases. Clearly, however, the outcome of that approach will depend entirely on the facts of the individual case."*

This confirmed cases for internal and external relocation should be treated the same, with the location of the proposed relocation simply forming part of the court's considerations when determining whether to grant the application.

The judgement of Re: C and same treatment of internal and external relocation cases was considered and affirmed in Re: K (a child) (international relocation: appeal against judge's finds of fact) [2016] EWCA Civ 931 [2016] All ER (D) 30 and AH v DT [2017] EWHC 36 (Fam) (which are covered in more detail in Chapter 4).

Although it is now well established that internal and external relocation cases should not be differentiated, child removal / abduction cases are treated differently.

Re: R (a child) (domestic abduction) [2016] EWCA Civ 1016 considered an application for internal child abduction. The Mother had unilaterally removed the children from Kent to the northeast of England. The Father informed the Mother he would be seeking the return of the child, however before he could do so she applied for and obtained a without notice Prohibited Steps Order, preventing the Father from removing the children from her care.

The Father's application for the return of the child was dismissed and he appealed. The Father's appeal referenced the guidance from Re: C, stating that under precedent the court should apply the same treatment of internal and external abduction cases, meaning the court would restore the status quo, ordering the return of the child to Kent.

The Father's appeal was dismissed. In considering the judgement of Re: C it was held that the Judge's intention was not to state internal and external cases were to be treated the same on every level, but that the child's welfare was to be the court's paramount consideration in all cases.

It was noted the Hague Convention did not apply for domestic cases and should not be applied by analogy. There is no automatic presumption that a child removed internally should be returned and the status quo restored.

CHAPTER EIGHT

THE HAGUE CONVENTION

The Impact of Brexit

On 31st January 2020 the UK left the European Union, with the transition period ending on 31st December 2020. This means from 1st January 2021 EU instruments no longer apply unless adopted.

The relevant legislation governing the UK's withdrawal is the European Union (Withdrawal) Act 2018, which became law on 26th June 2018 and the European Union (Withdrawal Agreement) which became law on 23rd January 2020.

The Government have repealed the Brussels IIA legislation which regulates the rules around jurisdiction, parental responsibility, child protection and abduction. Cases issued before 31st December 2020 will continue to proceed under EU rules, however those issued after this date will be governed by the laws of the relevant jurisdictions. This could also potentially mean disputes about which country holds jurisdiction. This also places an even greater emphasis on ensuring expert knowledge is obtained on the relevant law in any country to where children may be relocating, as it is no longer possible to rely on Brussels II for enforcement of any order made in the English and Welsh courts governing child arrangements, including their return.

The Hague Convention has been in force in the UK since 1st October 2015 when the EU acceded to it. Following the UK's departure from the EU the UK Government has joined the Hague Convention in its own right, and therefore this does continue to apply. Whilst the Hague Convention does address matters for cross-country enforcement there are some gaps which were previously filled by Brussels II. The UK has applied to accede to the Lugano convention which covers a number of the same provisions of Brussels Regulations, however the UK's application was rejected in July 2021.

At the time of writing, there are 89 member states, and the EU signed up to the Hague Convention. When looking at an external relocation, either as the applicant or respondent a key starting point is to look at whether the country of proposed relocation is a signatory to the Hague Convention. This will have a dramatic impact upon the enforceability of any order and the remedies available to the court in the event of a breach.

The Purpose of the Hague Convention

The purpose of the Hague Convention is clearly set out in the document itself, with the first paragraph confirming that any signatory to the convention is *"firmly convinced that the interests of children are of paramount importance in matters relating to their custody."* This is along the same lines of the Children Act legislation, and recognised guidance that the child's welfare is the court's paramount consideration. The document continues to state that; *"the member state is entering in to the convention with a desire to protect children from the effects of their wrongful removal or retention and to establish procedures for their prompt return to their state of habitual residence."* It should also be noted that as well as covering child abduction the Hague Convention also protects rights of access, ensuring continued contact with a parent in another member state.

The Hague Convention provides member states with a mechanism for cooperation for implementing and enforcing orders relating to children, ensuring the prompt return of wrongly removed or retained children and ensuring the rights of custody and access in one state are respected in another. Refer to article 1 of the convention for it's clear scope / objectives.

For children that have been unlawfully removed or retained, this is covered under article 3 of the convention. This provides a definition of when a removal or retention is considered 'wrongful' which in summary are; where the removal or retention is a breach of *"rights of custody"* which can apply to an individual, institution or any other body, and at the time of removal or retention those rights were exercised or would have been if it were not for the removal or retention. Putting this in to practice, this could mean where a parent fails to return with a child after being permitted to leave / remove from the jurisdiction for a specified period, or removes them from the jurisdiction without permission. This would include removal either contrary to a court order or where no court order has been made, resulting in a child abduction offence.

Article 5 provides the definition of 'rights of custody' and 'rights of access';

> *"Rights of custody" shall include rights relating to the care of the person of the child and, in particular, the right to determine the child's place of residence;*
>
> *"Rights of access" shall include the right to take a child for a limited period of time to a place other than the child's habitual residence.*

As outlined in article 4, the convention applies to any child who was habitually resident in a Contracting State immediately before any breach of custody or access rights. The convention does not apply once the child turns 16 years of age.

Further commentary and guidance on Rights of Custody can also be found in Paragraph 2.16 and 2.17 Practice Direction 12F Family Procedure Rules 2010.

Article 7 – Co-Operation of Member States

The purpose of the convention is to ensure co-operation between member states and Article 7 summarises what this co-operation' may look like. There is a non-exhaustive list provided within the article, but this includes;

- Discovering the whereabouts of a child;
- Preventing further harm to the child or prejudice to the parties;
- Securing the voluntary return of the child;
- The exchange of background information relating to the child;

- To provide information as to the law in the relevant states;
- To make arrangements to secure the return of the child or exercise of rights of access;
- To arrange for the provision of legal aid and advice;
- For states to keep each other informed and updated and eliminating any obstacles.

Legal Aid

It should be noted the above article makes provisions for Legal Aid being provided.

Following the Legal Aid, Sentencing and Punishment of Offenders Act (LASPO) 2012, this heavily restricted the availability of Legal Aid, requiring parties to provide evidence of domestic abuse or child abuse prior to funding being available in the majority of private law children cases. However, applications under the Hague Convention do not have such a requirement, with public funding being available irrespective of means and merits testing.

Regulation 5(1)(h) of The Civil Legal Aid (Financial Resources and Payment for Services) Regulations 2013 (SI 2013/480) states legal services are to be provided irrespective of a party's financial circumstances to any of the matters listed in section 17(1)(a) and (b) of Schedule 1, Part 1 of LASPO. The relevant section stating;

> *"17(1) Civil legal services provided in relation to—*
>
> *(a) an application made to the Lord Chancellor under the 1980 European Convention on Child Custody for the recognition or enforcement in England and Wales of a decision relating to the custody of a child;*
>
> *(b) an application made to the Lord Chancellor under the 1980 Hague Convention in respect of a child who is, or is believed to be, in England and Wales."*

Automatic eligibility for Legal Aid applies only to the applicant in a Hague Convention application. This does not extend to the respondent.

Further guidance on Legal Aid eligibility is contained in paragraph 2.5 Practice Direction 12F Family Procedure Rules 2010;

> *"If you think that your child has been brought to, or kept in, England or Wales, and your State is a State party to the 1980 Hague Convention, then you should get in touch with your own Central Authority who will help you to send an application for the return of your child to the Central Authority for England and Wales. However, you are not obliged to contact your own Central Authority. You may contact the Central Authority for England and Wales directly, or you may simply instruct lawyers in England or Wales to make an application for you. The advantage of making your application through the Central Authority for England and Wales if you are applying from outside the United Kingdom is that you will get public funding ('legal aid') to make your application, regardless of your financial resources."*

Central Authority

Throughout the convention there is reference to the 'Central Authority'. Central Authority is defined in paragraph 2.6 of Practice direction 12F Family Procedure Rules 2010. This states the Central Authority in England and Wales for the purposes of the Hague Convention is the Lord Chancellor. His duties shall be carried out by the International Child Abduction and Contact Unit (ICACU). Their contact details have changed from those contained in paragraph 2.7 and if making an application it is important to check to ensure the current contact details are used.

Chapter III – Return of the Child

Chapter III, Articles 8 – 20 relate to the return of a child unlawfully removed or retained.

As set out in Article 8, where an application is being made for the return of a child, this can be made to either the Central Authority of the child's habitual residence or the Central Authority of any other Contracting State. This lists the information that should be provided in any application.

Article 10 places an obligation on member states to take all appropriate measures to secure the voluntary return of the child which could include making a relevant court order.

The return of a child unlawfully removed or retained should take place expeditiously, with Article 11 requiring the Central Authority of a member state to have reached a decision within six weeks of issue, and should they not have done so they can be requested to provide a statement explaining the reasons for any delay.

If a child has been unlawfully retained or removed in a contracting state for less than a year than the Central Authority should order the return of the child. Where the child has been in the state for over 12 months, the Central Authority should still order the return unless it is demonstrated that the child has now settled in the new environment, (Article 12). This is subject to the contents of Article 13 which provides exceptions where the court should not order the immediate return of the child, including;

- The child being at 'grave risk' of physical or psychological harm, or placed in an intolerable situation if ordered to return; or

- At the time of removal or retention the applicant had consented to removal or retention or was not exercising their custody rights at the time of removal or retention; or

- The child objects to being returned and has attained an age and degree of maturity which is appropriate to take in their views.

Article 20 creates a further exemption, where the return of a child would be a breach of a party's human rights.

Article 15 states that before ordering the return of a child the Central Authority can require the applicant to obtain from the authority of the state of habitual residence of the child a declaration that the removal or retention was unlawful.

Chapter IV – Rights of Access

Article 21 governs contact / rights of access.

This confirms the convention applies not just to securing the return of a child but also the facilitation of contact between a child in a member state. This confirms there is no distinction between the terms of the order when looking at contact or the return of a child.

Procedure

The procedure for an application under the Hague Convention is covered in Practice Direction 12F Family Procedure Rules 2010. As noted above, if applying in England and Wales the application should be made through the Central Authority being the ICACU. This will trigger an automatic entitlement to Legal Aid. If applying for the return of a child whom has been removed from the UK an application can still be made to the ICACU, but this may then be transferred to the Central Authority in the jurisdiction where the child has been removed to.

Once receiving an application, the ICACU will then send the application to a solicitor from an approved list unless one has already been instructed.

An application should be made to the Principle Registry of the Family Division of the High Court due to the international element.

The application should be made on form C67 and paragraph 2.11 PD12F outlines the information that should be provided;

> *(a) the names and dates of birth of the children;*
>
> *(b) the names of the children's parents or guardians;*
>
> *(c) the whereabouts or suspected whereabouts of the children;*

(d) the interest of the applicant in the matter (e.g. Mother, Father, or person with whom the child lives and details of any order placing the child with that person);

(e) the reasons for the application;

(f) details of any proceedings (including proceedings not in England or Wales, and including any legal proceedings which have finished) relating to the children;

(g) where the application is for the return of a child, the identity of the person alleged to have removed or retained the child and, if different, the identity of the person with whom the child is thought to be.

A statement in support may also be provided setting out more information about the application and background.

The requirement in Article 11 to reach a decision within 6 weeks of issue of an application is also confirmed in paragraph 2.14 PD12F FPR 2010.

As well as the convention itself, practitioners should refer to the accompanying 'outline' document which provides a short two page summary about the purpose of the convention.

There is a clear distinction between how the court deal with applications to remove to Hague Convention and non-Hague Convention Countries. The Hague Convention is viewed as a strong method of enforcement and a safety net to secure the return of a child or enforce the terms of an order. Chapter 5 provides a number of case examples where the court have considered applications between Hague Convention and non-Hague Convention Countries.

CHAPTER NINE

WHERE ARE WE NOW AND WHERE ARE WE GOING? RECENT DECISIONS: SB V M [2021]

One of the most recently reported cases considering relocation is SB v M [2021] EWFC 49. Judgement was handed down by Judd DBE J on 14th June 2021 following a three-day final hearing between 10th – 12th May 2021.

This related to an application by the Mother who was seeking to relocate to Africa with the party's 12-year old son, N. The application to relocate was opposed by the Father. If the Mother's application was refused the Father was also seeking a child arrangements order for shared care of N.

Both parents were citizens of the African country, simply referred to as 'A' in the judgement, however they left country A, moving to another country referred to as 'B' when they were children, the Father when he was 11 and the Mother when she was 2. The parents moved to the UK in 2006 however N was born in country B and was a citizen of that country. Shortly after N's birth the parties separated and the Mother moved back to the UK. The Father followed shortly after this. The parents reconciled in 2012 but this only lasted for a short time before separating again.

The Mother had looked for a number of jobs in London without success and in July 2020, was offered a job with a multi-national company in country A in Africa. Upon telling the Father of her plans to relocate, the Father applied for a without notice prohibited steps order to prevent her removal with N.

There had been a history of litigation and court applications including in 2014 for a child arrangements order which was concluded by consent, and in 2016 when the Father applied for an increase of his time with N.

This again was concluded by consent. The Mother applied for an order preventing the Father making any further court applications for a period of 3 years. This was disposed of by consent, with both parties agreeing to make no court applications within the next 2 years. N had resided with his Mother, with her being his primary carer for the entirety of his life.

There was a high level of tension and animosity between the parties, and the judge was referred to email exchanges between them, both making a number of allegations about the other restricting their contact with N.

In giving evidence the Mother said that if she was not allowed to relocate this would be the equivalent of a slow and painful death sentence to her. She said she would be forced to remain in London, one of the most expensive cities in the world, with no job and little prospects of finding one given the economic and financial crisis. By contrast, the Mother said if she was given permission to relocate she would have a high quality of life full of possibility and culture.

The Father opposed the application stating this would have a detrimental impact upon his relationship with N, who he had been spending time with every weekend and additional time during the school holidays, since the previous child arrangements order was made in 2016. He raised concerns that if the Mother was permitted to relocate, he would not be able to continue the same level of contact and would be in difficulties in enforcing any level of contact as the Mother N would be in a non-Hague Convention country.

The Father also raised concerns about N's safety, stating country A was a violent and dangerous place.

He also raised concerns about the security of the Mother's job, stating the company she was going to work for was in financial difficulties and suggested the Mother had better job prospects in London.

A CAFCASS officer was instructed to undertake a report. In doing so she spoke to both parents, N and his teacher. The recommendation in the report was that the Mother's application to relocate should be refused due to the impact this would have upon N's time with his Father and recommended an extension in the Father's contact time from Thursday to Tuesday every other week and half of all school holidays.

In reporting N's comments, the CAFCASS officer reported the N had clearly given the prospect of moving some thought and provided a number of reasons as to why this might be a good thing, although was of the view this would be 'OK' rather than being positive about it. N did not believe the relationship with his Father would be effected. The CAFCASS officer was of the view N was uncomfortable talking about matters and being a source of disagreement between his parents. In considering the report Judd DBE J noted that the CAFCASS officer had only considered the impact the move would have upon N's relationship with his Father. This had not considered the wider issues relating to N's welfare and the impact upon the Mother if the application was refused. The report and recommendations were therefore considered to be on partial information only.

The court considered evidence in the form of reports from two experts; Dr. S an academic and expert in the legal system in Country A, and Dr. M who practices law in country A.

Dr. S was critical of the legal system in country A, describing this as being full of corruption and lacking independence, resources and training. He stated women in particular have difficulties in winning cases in some districts of the capital.

Dr. M advised that an order of the English courts could be enforced in country A and gave information on how this can be achieved. An addendum to the report was filed which suggested these matters were not usually brought before the court. There was no reference made as to how parents resolve disputes of this nature, nor the actual arrangements to enforce an order in the event of a breach.

In considering the relevant law, the approach from the case of Re F (A Child) (International Relocation Case) [2015] was confirmed;

1. The guidance of K v K [2011] applies and the only authentic principle is the welfare of the child;

2. There must be a heightened scrutiny of proposals that interfere with the relationship between the child and a parent as per Section 2A Children Act 1989;

3. The welfare checklist is relevant;

4. The guidance from Payne v Payne may be misleading unless viewed in its proper context which may held the judge identify potentially relevant issues;

5. The court must carry out a welfare analysis of each proposal, undertaking a holistic and non-linear comparative evaluation of all plans;

6. In additional to the Article 8 rights to a family life the court must factor in the rights of the child to maintaining a relationship and direct contact with both parents on a regular basis;

7. The court must take in to account the parent's Article 8 rights, but the child's Article 8 rights take priority;

8. The court must consider the proportionality of the interference with the Article 8 rights of the child and parents.

The judge then carried out an analysis, looking at the pros and cons of both of the options before the court, being that N relocated with the Mother and that he remained in the country.

The Mother's application was refused and in giving judgement the following points were made;

1. The Mother would get over the disappointment if permission was not granted to relocate;

2. The judge did not believe the Mother's employment prospects in the UK were as bleak as she was suggesting;

3. N's comments about being 'OK' with moving with his Mother was based on his Mother's wishes and was too you to fully

appreciate what life would be like living in country A and the lack of face to face contact with his Father;

4. N's physical and educational needs could be met in both county N and if he remained in the country and therefore this was not something that was given weight in the decision;

5. N's relationship with his Father is bound to be effected if he moved to country A, facetime contact does not make up for face to face contact, which N clearly enjoys, having spoken about going walking an cycling with his Father;

6. The changes for N if he were to move to country A would be quite substantial as he has been brought up in Europe, however he would probably adapt and settle with his Mother's support if he were to move. But if he were to remain in the country he would also be likely to do well and enjoy his life with his Mother and Father;

7. N is at an important age in his life and the involvement of both parents in his life will be important to him;

8. Under Article 12 the court have the power to make orders for contact;

9. Taking in to consider that N's welfare was the court's paramount consideration, and weighing up the two options presented by the parties the judge found the better option for N would be to remain in the country in order to have regular and frequent time with his Father, and therefore the Mother's application to relocate was refused;

10. The Father's contact was increase from Sunday to Monday as it was held a move from two nights to five was too much of a jump.

This judgement confirms that the key guidance still comes from the case of Re: F (A Child) (International Relocation Case) [2015] EWCA Civ 882. The judgement was also another blow for the Payne v Payne guidance, with this being referred to as potentially misleading, and the Judge not applying this in her decision.

CHAPTER TEN

CONCLUSION

It is now clearly established that applications to relocate should be determined using the same guidance, this coming from the case of Re: F (A Child) (International Relocation Case) [2015]. The only thing the court must consider is that the child's welfare is their paramount consideration. Any application to relocate should be based purely on what is best for the child. This includes considering and applying the Section 1(3) Children Act 1989 Welfare Checklist.

The guidance from Payne v Payne [2001] has gone from a checklist, to guidance, to now being treated with extreme caution. No decision has been made to state the guidance should not be applied and practitioners should still refer to it, but it should not form a key part of their argument.

When determining a relocation application the court must consider a holistic approach, carrying out a detailed analysis of all possible options before them. No preference or additional weighting or scrutiny should be made of the applicant parent's proposal.

There is a high level of judicial discretion, with the judge being able to determine what weighting they attached to each of the Re: F [2015] and welfare checklist guidance, however applying only some of the criteria, or failing to give consideration or reference to one of the proposals before the court is likely to be wrong and give grounds to appeal.

With applications to relocate, preparation is the key and before pursuing any court application there should be consideration and discussions to setting out a clean plan and proposal, not just in what the child's 'new life' would be like, but also how links will be maintained with their 'old life'.

Case precedent would suggest that it is rare for courts to refuse applications to internally relocate, however every case is judged on its individual circumstances, with the decision ultimately being driven by what is best for the child and their welfare.

Following the UK's departure from the EU, the UK has joined the Hague Convention in its own right which means the distinction between the treatment of Hague Convention and non-Hague Convention countries is likely to be unaffected. It is still to be seen whether there will be any impact upon relocation cases due to the UK no longer assigning to EU law, such as Brussels II and this is only likely to show over time.

Disputes involving children is often a highly emotive area of law, and applications to remove are often some of the most difficult before the court due to the long lasting and potentially permanent impact this will have on a child and their relationships. As the world returns to some sort of normality and travel and boarder restrictions relax following the COVID-19 pandemic, it is likely this is an area of law that is going to continue to become more common.

MORE BOOKS BY LAW BRIEF PUBLISHING

A selection of our other titles available now:-

'A Practical Guide to Solicitor and Client Costs – 2nd Edition' by Robin Dunne
'Constructive Dismissal – Practice Pointers and Principles' by Benjimin Burgher
'A Practical Guide to Religion and Belief Discrimination Claims in the Workplace' by Kashif Ali
'A Practical Guide to the Law of Medical Treatment Decisions' by Ben Troke
'Fundamental Dishonesty and QOCS in Personal Injury Proceedings: Law and Practice' by Jake Rowley
'A Practical Guide to the Law in Relation to School Exclusions' by Charlotte Hadfield & Alice de Coverley
'A Practical Guide to Divorce for the Silver Separators' by Karin Walker
'The Right to be Forgotten – The Law and Practical Issues' by Melissa Stock
'A Practical Guide to Planning Law and Rights of Way in National Parks, the Broads and AONBs' by James Maurici QC, James Neill et al
'A Practical Guide to Election Law' by Tom Tabori
'A Practical Guide to the Law in Relation to Surrogacy' by Andrew Powell
'A Practical Guide to Claims Arising from Fatal Accidents – 2nd Edition' by James Patience
'A Practical Guide to the Ownership of Employee Inventions – From Entitlement to Compensation' by James Tumbridge & Ashley Roughton
'A Practical Guide to Asbestos Claims' by Jonathan Owen & Gareth McAloon
'A Practical Guide to Stamp Duty Land Tax in England and Northern Ireland' by Suzanne O'Hara
'A Practical Guide to the Law of Farming Partnerships' by Philip Whitcomb

'Covid-19, Homeworking and the Law – The Essential Guide to Employment and GDPR Issues' by Forbes Solicitors

'Covid-19, Force Majeure and Frustration of Contracts – The Essential Guide' by Keith Markham

'Covid-19 and Criminal Law – The Essential Guide' by Ramya Nagesh

'Covid-19 and Family Law in England and Wales – The Essential Guide' by Safda Mahmood

'A Practical Guide to the Law of Unlawful Eviction and Harassment – 2nd Edition' by Stephanie Lovegrove

'Covid-19, Residential Property, Equity Release and Enfranchisement – The Essential Guide' by Paul Sams and Louise Uphill

'Covid-19, Brexit and the Law of Commercial Leases – The Essential Guide' by Mark Shelton

'A Practical Guide to Costs in Personal Injury Claims – 2nd Edition' by Matthew Hoe

'A Practical Guide to the General Data Protection Regulation (GDPR) – 2nd Edition' by Keith Markham

'Ellis on Credit Hire – Sixth Edition' by Aidan Ellis & Tim Kevan

'A Practical Guide to Working with Litigants in Person and McKenzie Friends in Family Cases' by Stuart Barlow

'Protecting Unregistered Brands: A Practical Guide to the Law of Passing Off' by Lorna Brazell

'A Practical Guide to Secondary Liability and Joint Enterprise Post-Jogee' by Joanne Cecil & James Mehigan

'A Practical Guide to the Pre-Action RTA Claims Protocol for Personal Injury Lawyers' by Antonia Ford

'A Practical Guide to Neighbour Disputes and the Law' by Alexander Walsh

'A Practical Guide to Forfeiture of Leases' by Mark Shelton

'A Practical Guide to Coercive Control for Legal Practitioners and Victims' by Rachel Horman

'A Practical Guide to Rights Over Airspace and Subsoil' by Daniel Gatty
'Tackling Disclosure in the Criminal Courts – A Practitioner's Guide' by Narita Bahra QC & Don Ramble
'A Practical Guide to the Law of Driverless Cars – Second Edition' by Alex Glassbrook, Emma Northey & Scarlett Milligan
'A Practical Guide to TOLATA Claims' by Greg Williams
'Artificial Intelligence – The Practical Legal Issues' by John Buyers
'A Practical Guide to the Law of Prescription in Scotland' by Andrew Foyle
'A Practical Guide to the Construction and Rectification of Wills and Trust Instruments' by Edward Hewitt
'A Practical Guide to the Law of Bullying and Harassment in the Workplace' by Philip Hyland
'How to Be a Freelance Solicitor: A Practical Guide to the SRA-Regulated Freelance Solicitor Model' by Paul Bennett
'A Practical Guide to Prison Injury Claims' by Malcolm Johnson
'A Practical Guide to the Small Claims Track' by Dominic Bright
'A Practical Guide to Advising Clients at the Police Station' by Colin Stephen McKeown-Beaumont
'A Practical Guide to Antisocial Behaviour Injunctions' by Iain Wightwick
'Practical Mediation: A Guide for Mediators, Advocates, Advisers, Lawyers, and Students in Civil, Commercial, Business, Property, Workplace, and Employment Cases' by Jonathan Dingle with John Sephton
'The Mini-Pupillage Workbook' by David Boyle
'A Practical Guide to Crofting Law' by Brian Inkster
'A Practical Guide to Spousal Maintenance' by Liz Cowell
'A Practical Guide to the Law of Domain Names and Cybersquatting' by Andrew Clemson
'A Practical Guide to the Law of Gender Pay Gap Reporting' by Harini Iyengar

'A Practical Guide to the Rights of Grandparents in Children Proceedings' by Stuart Barlow

'NHS Whistleblowing and the Law' by Joseph England

'Employment Law and the Gig Economy' by Nigel Mackay & Annie Powell

'A Practical Guide to Noise Induced Hearing Loss (NIHL) Claims' by Andrew Mckie, Ian Skeate, Gareth McAloon

'An Introduction to Beauty Negligence Claims – A Practical Guide for the Personal Injury Practitioner' by Greg Almond

'Intercompany Agreements for Transfer Pricing Compliance' by Paul Sutton

'Zen and the Art of Mediation' by Martin Plowman

'A Practical Guide to the SRA Principles, Individual and Law Firm Codes of Conduct 2019 – What Every Law Firm Needs to Know' by Paul Bennett

'A Practical Guide to Adoption for Family Lawyers' by Graham Pegg

'A Practical Guide to Industrial Disease Claims' by Andrew Mckie & Ian Skeate

'A Practical Guide to Redundancy' by Philip Hyland

'A Practical Guide to Vicarious Liability' by Mariel Irvine

'A Practical Guide to Applications for Landlord's Consent and Variation of Leases' by Mark Shelton

'A Practical Guide to Relief from Sanctions Post-Mitchell and Denton' by Peter Causton

'A Practical Guide to Equity Release for Advisors' by Paul Sams

'A Practical Guide to the Law Relating to Food' by Ian Thomas

'A Practical Guide to Financial Services Claims' by Chris Hegarty

'The Law of Houses in Multiple Occupation: A Practical Guide to HMO Proceedings' by Julian Hunt

'A Practical Guide to Unlawful Eviction and Harassment' by Stephanie Lovegrove

'Occupiers, Highways and Defective Premises Claims: A Practical Guide Post-Jackson – 2nd Edition' by Andrew Mckie

'A Practical Guide to Financial Ombudsman Service Claims' by Adam Temple & Robert Scrivenor
'A Practical Guide to Advising Schools on Employment Law' by Jonathan Holden
'A Practical Guide to Running Housing Disrepair and Cavity Wall Claims: 2nd Edition' by Andrew Mckie & Ian Skeate
'A Practical Guide to Holiday Sickness Claims – 2nd Edition' by Andrew Mckie & Ian Skeate
'Arguments and Tactics for Personal Injury and Clinical Negligence Claims' by Dorian Williams
'A Practical Guide to Drone Law' by Rufus Ballaster, Andrew Firman, Eleanor Clot
'A Practical Guide to Compliance for Personal Injury Firms Working With Claims Management Companies' by Paul Bennett
'A Practical Guide to Dog Law for Owners and Others' by Andrea Pitt
'RTA Allegations of Fraud in a Post-Jackson Era: The Handbook – 2nd Edition' by Andrew Mckie
'RTA Personal Injury Claims: A Practical Guide Post-Jackson' by Andrew Mckie
'On Experts: CPR35 for Lawyers and Experts' by David Boyle
'An Introduction to Personal Injury Law' by David Boyle
'A Practical Guide to Subtle Brain Injury Claims' by Pankaj Madan

These books and more are available to order online direct from the publisher at www.lawbriefpublishing.com, where you can also read free sample chapters. For any queries, contact us on 0844 587 2383 or mail@lawbriefpublishing.com.

Our books are also usually in stock at www.amazon.co.uk with free next day delivery for Prime members, and at good legal bookshops such as Wildy & Sons.

We are regularly launching new books in our series of practical day-to-day practitioners' guides. Visit our website and join our free newsletter to be kept informed and to receive special offers, free chapters, etc.

You can also follow us on Twitter at www.twitter.com/lawbriefpub.

www.ingramcontent.com/pod-product-compliance
Lightning Source LLC
LaVergne TN
LVHW022106200926
848481LV00003B/1071
9781914608063